T0382171

CONVERGING PATHS

CONVERGING PATHS

by

E. T. CAMPAGNAC

Professor of Education in the University of Liverpool
formerly one of His Majesty's Inspectors of Schools

Cambridge :
at the University Press
1916

CAMBRIDGE
UNIVERSITY PRESS

University Printing House, Cambridge CB2 8BS, United Kingdom

Cambridge University Press is part of the University of Cambridge.

It furthers the University's mission by disseminating knowledge in the pursuit of
education, learning and research at the highest international levels of excellence.

www.cambridge.org
Information on this title: www.cambridge.org/9781107475236

© Cambridge University Press 1916

This publication is in copyright. Subject to statutory exception
and to the provisions of relevant collective licensing agreements,
no reproduction of any part may take place without the written
permission of Cambridge University Press.

First published 1916
First paperback edition 2014

A catalogue record for this publication is available from the British Library

ISBN 978-1-107-47523-6 Paperback

Cambridge University Press has no responsibility for the persistence or accuracy of
URLs for external or third-party internet websites referred to in this publication,
and does not guarantee that any content on such websites is, or will remain, accurate
or appropriate.

PREFACE

THE study of Education is the study of the
ideals of men and of the methods which they
have pursued in making towards their ideals. The
methods bear many different names, and in their
nature differ one from another; the ideals, by
whatever titles known, draw their several companies
of adherents into a kindred, faintly acknowledged,
or happily owned, or by vehement protest of
denial made patent to the world. Akin they are,
but not identical: for, even if it is to one and
the same city that, from many quarters and by
many converging paths, the travellers are brought
together at last, they give to it, each one of them
and each group of them, something of the quality
both of their starting-place and of the way along
which they journeyed. Their destination is as
individual as themselves, for indeed it was to find
themselves that they set forth; and yet it is not

with surprise or indignation, that discovering themselves arrived, they discover familiar strangers and dear antagonists, assembled like themselves at that elusive and unique and common goal.

The chapters which make up this book are intended to illustrate this theme.

E. T. C.

LIVERPOOL
March 1916

TABLE OF CONTENTS

Τῷ δ' ἐν ἡμῖν θείῳ ξυγγενεῖc εἰcὶ κινήcειc αἱ τοῦ
παντὸc διανοήcειc καὶ περιφοραί. ταύταιc δὴ ξυνεπόμενον
ἕκαcτον δεῖ .... τῷ κατανοουμένῳ τὸ κατανοοῦν ἐξομοι-
ῶcαι κατὰ τὴν ἀρχαίαν φύcιν, ὁμοιώcαντα δὲ τέλοc ἔχειν
τοῦ προτεθέντοc ἀνθρώποιc ὑπὸ θεῶν ἀρίcτου βίου πρόc
τε τὸν παρόντα καὶ τὸν ἔπειτα χρόνον.

PLATO, Timaeus, 90 D.

Εἰ καὶ cοὶ ἑδραῖοc ἀεὶ βίοc, οὐδὲ θάλαccαν
   ἔπλωc χερcαίαc τ' οὐκ ἐπάτηcαc ὁδούc,
Ἔμπηc Κεκροπίηc ἐπιβήμεναι, ὄφρ' ἂν ἐκείναc
   Δήμητροc μεγάλαc νύκταc ἴδῃc ἱερῶν,
Τῶν ἄπο κὴν ζωοῖcιν ἀκηδέα, κεῦτ' ἂν ἵκηαι
   ἐc πλεόνων, ἕξειc θυμὸν ἐλαφρότερον.

Anth. Pal. xi. 42.

The necessities of the present and the ideals of the future
are both related to the past. An ideal shaped by present
necessity alone is always untrue to permanent relations.
An attempt to meet present necessities shaped only by an
ideal is always untrue to fact and baseless. The past is
at once the cause of the present and the womb of the
possibilities of the future.

F. J. A. HORT, The Way, the Truth, the Life,
Macmillan, 1894, p. 201.

CHAPTER I

If we are to discuss Religious Instruction with any advantage, we must attempt some definitions. We must determine what we mean by Instruction and by Religion: the first is a hard word, the second harder.

By religion I shall here intend the sense of mystery; the search for the heart of mystery and the discovery for ourselves of relationships, personal, intimate, with mystery, which still eludes us as our knowledge advances; the government of conduct and the ordering of affairs in the light of these relationships, coloured by experience and hardened by commerce with the world; and finally the emerging harmony of the mysterious with the actual, the constructive destruction of the barriers between two realms.

Much as men differ from their fellows in experience, and in the account which they give of experience, in this at least they are at one. They all make a distinction between the region of knowledge and the region, variously named, of whatever lies beyond knowledge. The distinction is important; for it affords the most common, and indeed the universal, mode of a great affirmation, namely, that there are two regions: that of knowledge, and another; and that of both we are in some sort aware. If the horizon is drawn with a vast compass, its encircling boundaries, wide as they may be, do not limit the range of the spirit which is urged by fearful adventure or hazardous hope beyond their confines; or if a man's life seems to be spent within a clear, bright circle of illumination, the vividness of the light makes sharp the edges of an unknown and invisible region, with which he claims the beginnings of acquaintance by saying that he does not know it. Or, if instructed by our climate, and set in half lights and transparent mists, we can claim neither the broad spreading horizon upon the verge of which the eye falls in weariness to dreams, nor the vivid contrast of light with darkness, we may yet find in the demesne of our thought what at all seasons an English landscape offers: a certain shy clearness revealing itself fitfully, and as fitfully withdrawing behind a veil of romantic obscurity; like the bloom blurring and enriching outlines upon which eye and imagination rest; like the warm breath of cold October fields; the cold vapour which drapes and designs the form of summer meadows; the netted shadows of leaves still or tremulous, rent by a sudden gust, and settling once more upon the ground; the other element, neither water nor air, which lies upon the surface of water and supports the air, dividing, uniting, hiding, interpreting both.

The ordered progression of the seasons marking through time their timeless course may not turn the accustomed mind to speculation; but the strange unkindness of a November day in summer, the ravishing touch of June falling upon February, sting us with the sense of mystery, not less than the varying moods (not to be foretold or explained) of friends showing beneath the even surface of gentle use sharp edges of anger, or the bewildering benefactions of foes who break with shrewd gentleness through the armour we had provided against blows.

To reflect is to catch the image of mystery upon the mirror of imagination. The plain routine of life is for the busiest or the most unreflecting of men broken by some moments of pause, when retrospect and anticipation confirm and suggest the sense of unknown powers as of palpable but invisible presences controlling human destiny. The fragile beauty of children; the increasing powers of youth, touched with a finer delicacy than that of childhood, and strangely roughened—not yet by hard contact with the world, but by the eruption upon its surface of primeval barbarisms and savageries; the gathered strength of maturity engaged with itself and with the world in the effort to fashion and mould to an enduring shape the now chastened and corrected hopes of earlier years; and age at length, if age be attained, sustaining with dignity or dishonour the last indignity or final honour of death—these are all phases of an unchanging movement, a fragment, even when it seems to be complete, and yet how

rarely completed even in semblance! For the un-
earthly charm of infancy is crushed, the hope of
youth baffled, the labour of maturity entangled in
futility and despair, and age, if age arrives, overtaken at length by the pursuing, relentless fate.

So men have contemplated the course of human
affairs, and felt, for all their reluctance to admit its
presence, and the more keenly for their hostility
towards it, the pressure of the mystery which surrounds them. Not less have others, whose language
and philosophy are more sanguine and hopeful, been
possessed by the same sense. If to crown happiness or
to assuage sorrow they cast themselves upon something which is more than either sorrow or happiness, it
is because within experience and as a part of it they
recognise the two realms of the known and the unknown, and mark the firm boundaries of the known
by the luminous frontiers of what they cannot see.

We are not to suppose that children are unaware
of mysterious presences, or unvisited by them.
Surrounded by the walls of their homes, by their
gardens, or by the streets in which they live; en-
compassed by their kindred, their friends, their
teachers and other persons with whom they have to
do, they cast their eyes, with their minds, beyond
the enclosure in which they are penned, and make
rich conjectures upon what lies without it. The
conversation of grown people, heard and imperfectly
understood; the contrast between their own strength
so valiantly displayed, and the concealed and silent
strength of people whose mere weight would overbear

them; the consciousness that such freedom as they enjoy is granted by an authority which could withhold it—bring them sharply to the sense of mystery, sharply, and yet not always harshly or with pain, since they take for granted their limitations, and, without words, make through them their irresistible claim upon strength and knowledge which they do not themselves possess. For them, weakness is often the pledge of support, and their inability to take care of themselves itself the assurance that others should take care of them. But at times their security is invaded by loneliness suddenly clutching at their hearts. A twig breaking noiselessly from a bough and falling before their feet upon the garden path; the quick intrusion of a stranger who is not expected; the bark of a dog; the whistle of a railway train—may fill them with terror, and for the moment cut for them the lines of communication between their own minds and the minds of those in whom they trust.

The communication may be quickly restored, as when the sudden tightening of a child's hand as you hold it reveals to you his fear, and to him your presence, which for that immeasurable instant of alarm he had forgotten. But at night, the light that falls on closed eyelids and is gone again, the creaking of a board in the floor, the rustle of a curtain, renew and prolong for a time which is not accurately measured in minutes the sense of desolation.

And, once more, the sense of mystery is quickened by mere curiosity; to traverse an unfamiliar field, to open a locked cupboard, to explore the winding stairs of a tower, is for them to lay their hand with happy hesitation upon the half-feared, half-welcomed unknown.

Physiologists, I am told, have measured the interval which elapses between the receipt of stimulus and the despatch of response. The higher the organism, the more fully charged is this interval. Experience is not the acceptance, but the interpretation of whatever fortune bestows. We may speak in a figure of the sadness of a tree shrivelled by too keen a wind, or of the happiness of a stream lightly touched by the breeze, but it is a figure which goes beyond what fact can warrant. For us, pain and pleasure are derived from reflection upon the blow or the caress received; it is the treasured image of the fact, not the fact, which moves us. A child quickly interrupted in the process which leads to reflection will not cry at a bruise, for though his body is hurt, we have come too adroitly to his aid for the injury to touch his mind. And so again a child surfeited with things intended by ignorant benevolence to please him, feels no pleasure, for he has not time to reflect on his possessions. It is only when we think, and not before, that we discover, as in a flash revealed to the inward eye, the wealth which has been brought to us. Significance is always spiritual.

But we shall come short of the truth and do violence to the sincere philosophy of children, if we find in significance an escape, as some misnamed idealists call it, from reality. It is not an escape; it is rather a return to the real and the material, which, lit with meaning, take on a new and imperishable value; facts, made significant, stand in their place in the order of time, or we may say, keep their rank in the unceasing procession of events, but cast on them, or some of them, the contiguous or the kindred, a generous light which lifts them too into an eternal sequence. If it is urged, by way of objection, that this reflection is rare, we may readily agree, for a series is no less a series if it be intermittent: day follows day in a succession which no man calls broken because night after night the darkness blots out the sun. Indeed, as without interposed silences, without steps taken and halts made, no melody could come of sound, no course be pursued, so always a series to be maintained must be marked and punctuated by intervals of cessation. Or if again, it is more keenly urged that the intervals between facts made significant are at once too frequent, too long and too irregular, we may acquiesce, for here again we are driven upon the contrast between the understood and the unintelligible. What we cannot understand we suffer; what we bring within the circle of reflection, we may be properly said to experience. It is significance which changes routine to ritual, and every ritual endows outward things with permanence by revealing within them a spirit, content with a certain ironic modesty to enshrine itself in forms, which it nevertheless transcends. Children who transform a

table to a stage-coach, and chairs to horses, do not
cease to use the table and the chairs; they interpret
them; they do not interpret them *away*. And when
later the things they used for their high purposes are
abandoned, or seem to be abandoned, it is not
because they did not fitly body forth the children's
ideas, but that larger ideas have claimed a fresh
representation, a nobler and a subtler spirit a new
incarnation. For all ideas spring to birth in flesh,
and keep their radiance within the body which they
transfigure.

The common, reiterated observance of a form,
a ceremonial of the nursery, the schoolroom or the
playground, wonderfully unites those who keep it.
But it is a barrier between them and others. To
those who cannot understand it, children will not
deign to expound it; more than this, they will not
even grant that those who share their celebration,
find in it, all of them, the same central meaning.
Mystics at heart, children jealously guard their
fierce solitude.

Yet solitude itself has its boundaries, and the
heart speaking to itself strikes echoes from its own
walls. The colloquy, reverberant through the silent
dwelling of the lonely mind, becomes intolerable for
its poignancy, and other persons, different of course,
and unable quite perfectly to comprehend, are sought
for company. Shaken by their vehement joys and
by their passionate sufferings (so slight if we judge
them by their apparent causes, yet edged by so
sharp an anguish for themselves) children turn from

excess of loneliness and to allay the ardour of their
burning emotions to others, even to ourselves, con-
fident of a sympathy which shall be sincere, if
inadequate, and perhaps the more comfortable and
sustaining for its very dullness. We render then at
least the exquisite service of dolls or toys held close
in the dark, of dogs against which they can press
their faces; it may be that, at best, in an ampler
silence, or in the inarticulate sounds of understanding
and companionship which children draw even from
natures hard with shyness, or perhaps in rare,
unpremeditated words, we give them something
more nearly matched with the exigent demands of
their happiness or their pain.

More nearly matched, but not equal to their
need will be what we offer. Much we may do; all
we cannot do, and, if we are wise, shall not attempt.

High emotion of whatever sort, whether of
sorrow or of delight, brings loneliness; or, it may
be more accurately said, high emotion has loneliness
as a part of its very essence. Hence the supreme
difficulty of human communication. We long to
share with others, and especially with our friends,
what we prize most highly ourselves, and they,
for their part, are willing to share whatever may
be communicable; but the heart of emotion can
never be fully shared, and we become aware of the
bonds of kindred and sympathy most certainly
when they serve also as fetters and restraints upon
expression where expression would injure and even
profane. Thus again, but at a higher level, we are

driven upon solitude, but a solitude no longer
bounded by unyielding walls of incomprehension,
nor even by the circling pressure of friends who in
part, but only in part, take our meaning. We have
made our appeal, and in making it gone beyond the
range and province of our judges; our voice travels
further into a void from which it can call no echo;
we are alone, not in a crowd, but in a universe. It
is then that the religious instinct, dormant at first,
gradually awakening in the increasing and engrossing
affairs of men with men, breaks at length into full
vitality; it is then that speech finds its response in
the infinite silence, and emotion becomes operative
and fruitful in a mind which, contemplating itself,
sees a diviner mind; then—to use the language of
St Paul—it apprehends that by which also it is
apprehended.

We shall probably not be accused of judging
human nature too harshly, if we say that few minds
can sustain themselves for long periods at this
altitude. They fall, out of sheer fatigue, to lower
and easier levels, and here for the most part they
reside. But the mind having once ascended to the
height at which solitude blooms into speech with
the Infinite, and discovered its counterpart in the
eternal, bears always some token by which it is
known. It may be a certain sweetness, as of a
breath borne mysteriously through airless streets
from clean fields and the sea; or it may be a certain
detachment from affairs, a detachment which no one
need mistake for indifference. It may be a certain

resetting of values; commonly it is a limping gait which marks the man who has encountered his Maker. Indeed, to prolong the period of the spirit's exaltation has something of the indelicacy and stupidity of an exquisite visit at a friend's house stretched out beyond the just moment for departure. The charm which we sought to maintain and immortalise is dulled and lost, and even memory cannot retain a semblance of its brief vivid beauty. To return to the ordinary avocations of men, not without a sense of discrepancy, and yet with a resolute and unaffected intention to accept the reality of them without denying the rare and transcendent reality of that other remembered period; to reconcile these two and to bring them back (for it is a restoration which we desire) to their primitive and natural harmony—this is the last test, and the highest triumph of the religious spirit.

But what of teaching, or instruction? Religion, that living system of fetters voluntarily assumed to tie men to a certain mode of life, is built upon an assumption which the progress of that life confirms. That assumption is the fact of relationship, permanent always, conscious at times, of the human spirit with another spirit which it names divine. It is at least the fact that at all times, and in all places, there have been some persons who have made this assumption and acted upon it. That, at any rate, is beyond dispute; though it may be disputed, as it is in fact disputed, whether that assumption was initially justified, or is supported by experience.

It might, I think, be reasonably argued that even
to raise the question is in a sense to admit the
assumption, but I do not propose to argue now in
that way. Instruction about religion might be
given by persons who did not themselves make the
assumption of which I have spoken, but who know,
just as they might know other historical facts, that
the assumption had indeed been made, and is still
made, by many men. Even for a fantastic rationalist, an academic Malvolio, this assumption, though
he did not share it, could not but have weight, and
I can imagine a man very scrupulous to give due
weight to it for the very reason that it was not an
assumption which justified itself in his own eyes.
A subtler criticism than I can here attempt might
portray such a character, and trace the movements
of his mind as he sought to be honest to himself, his
subjects and his pupils. To present to other minds
what one does not believe, while acquiescing in the
fact that other people believe it, and after offering
evidence, the best that may be obtained, upon either
side of a debated question, to leave one's listeners to
decide for themselves, is a performance which demands praise, not only for the intellectual force
which it exhibits, but for the remarkable moral
restraint which it attests.

Attractive as such a figure may be as a theme
for some philosophic essayist, we must for the
present leave him with expressions of respect and
of goodwill, and the hope of meeting him again.

Now we must rather concern ourselves with

people who not only know the astounding assumption to which our attention has been led, but have made it themselves, or with those who imagine that they have made it. It is very easy to suppose that a current belief is our own belief. We accept a traditional language, we adopt a conventional behaviour, we do not question that we entertain the view which others apparently entertain, and which we seem ourselves to entertain, until at last we are challenged by some crucial test. The course of life provides many such a test, and none of them is perhaps sharper and more decisive than that with which we are confronted when we are called upon to give instruction upon a theory commonly held— held by the best people, held in such a fashion that there is a kind of effrontery in not seeming to hold it, and yet after all a theory which we have not made our own.

Teachers whose business it is to deal with other subjects, sometimes discover at the outset of their career, and sometimes later in its course, that for their own part they have no vital knowledge of the many things which they are expected to teach to others; that history, or geography, or English literature, has less sap and savour for them than an apple, a pear, or a beefsteak; and in happy instances the impulse of their pupils' minds drives them to a position which they ought long ago to have made their starting point. But there are others who neither bring to their work, nor find as it proceeds, knowledge of this sort. They cannot communicate what they do not possess. Instruction about religion they may give; they may be lucid in their treatment of the geography of Palestine, and in their handling of the Chronicles, they may assign dates and authors to the Psalms, they may blend history with geography in their schedule of St Paul's missionary journeys, or even make classifications of the Miracles—but religious teaching they will not give, for religious teaching is teaching full of religion, teaching which fosters religious life.

Such teachers as these we may dismiss from our consideration, and turn now to those who seem well equipped for giving religious teaching. They are themselves religious persons; they have, if but for a moment, seen the things of which they might speak. Will they speak of them? Shall we complain if they take, or seem to take, the attitude either of a disinterested and speculative rationalist, or of the conventional person unlit with religious illumination, who repeats without emotion words which for him recall no emotion—shall we complain if men do not wear their hearts upon their sleeves, and treat as one of the commodities of the scholastic market place the secret treasure of their spirits? Shall we complain if, for fear their voices should dull their pupils' ears to the unutterable speech of the spirit, they maintain an obstinate and even passionate silence? We shall complain if they give to their pupils less than their best, and we shall easily convict them of an ingenuous inconsistency; for all their teaching if they be such persons as we have supposed, will be religious—that is to say, it will bear the impress which has stamped itself in indelible marks upon the whole of their nature. They will not, of course, drag disconcerting morals into their ordinary lessons, they will not exhort their pupils to be accurate in arithmetic or precise in grammar in the name of honesty and truth, but, without speaking of truth or honesty, they will assure those who hear them that there are such things, and that they are of supreme moment.

They will exhibit in their manner a sobriety and a gentleness which characterise those whose minds are not set upon the pursuit of popularity or success. They will give the impression of a reserve of strength, of possessing stores from which they draw at need. It will be clear that where their treasure is their heart is also. If their work is done in this country, it will be for them to take their pupils through various parts of the Bible, and whatever else they may say, or omit to say, about the books which are prescribed for study, they will make it plain that here we have, garnered within a single volume, the most varied, the most intimate, and the most convincing records of the speech of man with God. They will be scrupulous not to over-emphasise; indeed, they will avoid emphasis altogether; but they will read to children the story of God walking in the garden, of man discovering Him there, with a surprise which cannot be distinguished from expectation; the legends of the children of men set back as it were by a generation from their divine ancestry, and from time to time forgetting their origin. They toil and find their labour rewarded, and rejoice in the fruits of their work. They toil again, and the labour of days and of wakeful nights is frustrated. And then they turn in recollection, they cry out for help and receive it. They increase in wisdom and in possessions, and then fall like children into tired sleep, frightened of the dark, but presently consoled, for they and their people are guarded by a power which neither slumbers nor sleeps. They learn to confront pain with cheerfulness, and death without fear.

The religious teacher will need to offer no commentary upon these records. On rare occasions— and in general I think we may say, the better the man the more rare will be those occasions for him— he may desire to speak in his own words, even though in choosing them he is well aware that he uses words themselves less charged with dignity, and necessarily unsupported by tradition and ceremonial use. To one or two of his pupils he might speak, but the presence of a class checks his utterance. Some things are to be spoken in the ear, even though they might quite appropriately be whispered to many different people. It is only long experience, and special gifts, disciplined by the canons of a most exacting style, which will enable a man to address an audience, even if that audience be a familiar class, as if he were speaking severally to each person in it. A boarding school offers more and better opportunities for the establishment of personal relationships between teachers and pupils, than day

schools. Teachers, for all that may be said in
popular discussion, never stand, and never *can*
stand, in the position of parents. They have no
right to such a position, and grossly mistake both
their powers and their duties when they attempt to
adopt it. Yet teachers in boarding schools come
nearer to such a position than for the most part
teachers in day schools can hope to come.

It is sometimes supposed that parents find it
easy to talk to their children about important
matters of many kinds, and especially about religious
matters, which cannot easily or conveniently be
dealt with by the teacher. On the contrary, the
more intimate parents are with their children, the
less they talk. There may be sudden and unexpected
moments of speech upon high themes, but in general,
home conversation is about wet boots, dirty collars,
or inkstained handkerchiefs, of food eaten too fast,
or toys left untidily on the floors, about getting up
in the morning and going to bed at night, and not
teasing the cat. This is the language which we use
with our children; more than this, they overhear
our conversation with our contemporaries of a
concert, a dinner party, a country hotel, the odd
perversity of the gardener and the irregular habits
of the men who clean the windows. More rarely
they hear talk of politics, of books, of pictures.
Sometimes, though seldom, some question of right
or wrong is debated. The children listen and take
little part. They do not hear; they rather overhear; and they note with far more attentive an

interest our manner as we deal with these topics, than the course of our arguments or the conclusions which we reach. They overhear. It may be, with a subtler sense they also overhear a different and a finer conversation. They may remark a silence which overtakes speech when it attempts a theme too lofty for words. They may detect us in certain acts of reverence; they may be aware that behind our irritation we preserve some kindness; behind our follies, some wisdom; behind our conventions and artifices, some sincerity. They may perhaps discover that though most of our conversation ranges upon the level of the streets, some of it may be said, in language not less true than poetic, to be in heaven. If that were so, they would be getting religious instruction.

CHAPTER II

COMMERCIAL EDUCATION

Man cannot live by bread alone. But some bread he must have; more than a certain amount he cannot eat; with none he dies.

Bread, then, he must get: the question is *how*? This appears at first to be the only question; yet when he attempts to answer it, certain other questions arise, and will not be silenced: they claim their answers before they will suffer the first—what seemed to be the only—question to be answered. One of these important questions is—"Bread—for what purpose?" and another is—"Bread—of what kind?" We may find that these two are but different forms of the same problem.

For what purpose do we seek bread? What is food for? It is to restore spent energies, to repair wasted tissues, to maintain life. The answer is correct, yet unsatisfactory. No healthy person eats his food for these reasons: he eats his food because he likes it, because he enjoys the process of eating it. And the more completely unconscious he is of everything except his liking and enjoyment, the

more keenly he likes and enjoys, and the more
perfectly the ignored purpose is fulfilled.

Bread of what kind? Food of what quality?
Simple text-books of hygiene tell us what chemical
or other properties it should combine. But no
healthy man ordering a meal, no wholesome house-
wife providing for her family, dreams of consulting
the books. We choose what we have a taste for
at the time. Experience has indeed taught us to
forecast our tastes with tolerable accuracy. A sugared
cake offered at breakfast would be a cruel jest; soup
would be an insult at the hour when we expect tea;
the matutinal rasher an affront to the dinner table.
We pleasantly contrive to gratify the tastes we know
and can anticipate; we stoutly refuse to provide for
a self-conscious digestive system.

The problem grows in complexity and fascination.
It is clear we eat because we like food and enjoy
eating: clear, no less, that we eat what we like;
but we do not always like food of the same sort.
True, the variations fall into a certain routine; the
changes mark the progress of a changeless ritual;
one dinner is much like another; the breakfast of
to-day asserts an undisputed kindred with the
breakfast of yesterday, and sends a silent, prophetic
greeting to the morrow's breakfast, which will not
repudiate the alliance nor fail the tradition. But
breakfast is never dinner; luncheon will not be
mistaken for tea. We cling to change with the
loyal and tenacious grasp with which we hold
custom itself.

It is not hard to find or to state the principle which governs these changes. The kind of food is determined by the state of the man just before he takes it. It were not more inept to offer a man a stone when he has asked for an egg, than to give him hot cocoa when he desires iced lemonade. The man has been hurrying along a dusty road on an August afternoon: iced lemonade is determined by that fact; he has had a long journey in February over branch lines of several ill-adjusted, rival railway companies: iced lemonade, though an excellent beverage on other occasions, is not for him to drink; the conditions prescribe cocoa. Beefsteak may in general be called food; and so may calves-foot jelly—indeed the two have a special intimacy of kinship: but neither is food for a particular man upon the particular occasion when he wants the other; and what he wants is decided by his condition at that time.

A man may be hungry, and food, we know, satisfies hunger. But unless a man is starving he will not take any food without considering its nature. Normal hunger allows discrimination; the normally hungry man satisfies his hunger with the foods which are appropriate to the special kind of hunger which he feels. When we say that a man has earned his dinner, we mean that he is—as the result of certain abstinences and activities—in a condition to eat it. If breakfast had never ceased, he would not be in that condition; if he had slept soundly and without interruption since breakfast, he would not be in that condition.

We have used the word "earn": we were led to it in our discussion of food, of hunger and its satisfaction. But we have used it in a sense, familiar indeed, and yet not the most usual. We give rein to a modest fancy when we say that a man earns his dinner: we seem to be unvisited by fancy, if we say that he earns his wages: even if we say he earns his salary, we have used a word which has unhappily lost its savour. Had it kept its savour, we should have saved our wit, and the problem of Commercial Education might have solved itself.

For what, after all, is Education? In its widest sense, it is the sum of all the activities by which a community seeks to express, to attain, and to enrich its ideal of life. It is unfortunate that a general statement such as this provokes almost universal ridicule: for a general statement, if it is true, is the form in which a general idea takes shape, and a general is a governing idea. It is reasonable to test the truth of a general idea, to reject it if it fails under examination: it is not reasonable to despise it because it claims to be general. Let this statement serve as a general statement—or let those who will provide another. Accepting this statement, we may then more narrowly, but in the light of our general definition further define Education as certain special activities or experiences which the Community selects and arranges for its younger members. Whatever else they miss, in whatever accidental order they may acquire other experiences, there are certain experiences and activities which the

Community decides that its younger members shall not miss, but shall receive in a certain order. But whether defined generally or more narrowly, Education has for its end life, a social life in which each member of a Community has his share.

The special activities, or groups of activities, which Education in its narrowest sense prescribes and provides for the young, need not be the same for all; but whatever they are, and however various, they must all contribute to the general end of Education—life; and life we are ready to declare is not sustained by bread alone.

Commercial Education is, with us in England at any rate, suspect. It is, indeed, smitten on both cheeks. Some of its critics decry it for seeking bread, an object with which the human spirit cannot be content; others maintain that it fails in its search, that even bread it cannot supply; others again, in appearance more severe, at heart more gentle, press both objections against it at once: they say that it is neither commercial nor educative.

"Misery acquaints a man with strange bedfellows"; Commercial Education is "not all alone unhappy." There is a melancholy pleasure in remarking that the same or like criticisms are directed against other special forms of Education. Classical Education, for instance, has not escaped. There are not wanting critics who entertain and boldly utter the belief that a "classical" training such as our schools and colleges have long given, not unchallenged but unchecked, falls something

short of Education; while others, armed with sharp
paradox, say that it equips us with a very imperfect
knowledge of the Classics.

Most men must do some work to get a living.
If Society is concerned in their living, if their life
is a part of the life of Society itself, then it may
fairly be argued that Society is also concerned in
their work. But if we claim from Society that it
should concern itself in the work of its members,
i.e. in the means they use to get their living, these
means must be of a kind that Society can approve,
they must themselves be forms of activity in which
Society expresses, reaches and improves its own
ideal of a social life. For his own sake, and for the
sake of Society, a man must not sacrifice his life for
his living.

An unsound distinction has been made, with
unhappy results, between technical and liberal
education. A technical education is held to be one
which teaches the methods of earning a living in
some special field of human activity: a liberal
education is supposed to give what is called culture.
A classical education has been taken as the only, or
as the most, liberal education. Yet for how large a
proportion of those who after school and college days
"keep up" their Greek and Latin, Greek and Latin
are stock in trade: nine-tenths of them are teachers.
And in this respect their training has been just as
technical as the training of plumbers. Classical
scholars, it might further be maintained, perform
less constant and less fundamental services to

Society than plumbers. Without gas pipes and drains, where would our modern civilisation be? Besides, plumbers as a class have, notoriously, a subtle and penetrating humour.

It may, it is true, be said that to teach a boy or a young man classics is not to give him a technical training, because it has not been customary to teach him how to use what he has learnt, how, in fact, to teach others. If this view be adopted, so far as earning a living goes, the classically trained man is not in a better, but in a worse case, than the plumber.

There are three main considerations to be held in mind:

(1) The work which a human being does to earn his living must not damage his humanity:

(2) The living which a human being earns must not injure his life:

(3) The wages of work (for convenience symbolised by money, but not to be identified with money) must be what food is to the healthily-hungry body—provision for restoring and augmenting vitality.

Some, though not all, of the complaints made against our schools, would be withdrawn if these considerations were allowed their proper weight. But, it must be added, if these considerations were allowed their proper weight, both the curriculum and the methods of our schools would be in some respects modified.

The consideration of general principles fatigues even an athletic mind. Let us attempt to be what

is called "practical." Employers declare that the
boys and young men whom they receive from our
schools and colleges into their firms lack both
qualities and elements of knowledge which they
ought to possess; and for want of which they fail
to satisfy their superiors and to achieve promotion
for themselves.   It is fair to ask them two questions:
what are the qualities, and what are the kinds of
knowledge which they desiderate?   It is fair, also,
to ask them at what age they expect boys or young
men to show themselves possessed of these qualities
and elements of knowledge.

At a time not even now very remote, children of
six and seven years of age were employed in coal-
mines.   No doubt, their practical experience created
and fostered in them qualities and gave to them
knowledge, at that early age or within a few years,
which were useful to themselves *as miners* and
profitable to their employers *as mine-owners*.   In
many other occupations the age of entrance was,
100 or 50 or 25 years ago, lower than it is to-day.
What was the reason of the change which has been
effected?   It is not that children could not work
at that tender age; not that their work was com-
mercially unprofitable (though in some cases it
proved to be so); it was that such work done at
that age robbed the children of the chance of adequate
development as human beings.

The early employment of children in coal-mines
stirred the imagination, not of people who cared for
mines, but of people who cared for children; or if

it stirred the mine-owners, it was not as mine-owners, but as men interested more deeply in their country, or in humanity, than in commercial success.

The slow tendency of educational legislation has been to raise the age of school-leaving for children; and this legislation is due mainly to the assertion of the same principle which prevented the early employment of children in mines. It was believed that by a prolonged attendance at schools they would be enriched as children, as human beings, and that through them the State would be enriched in a higher and completer humanity.

Has popular education, reorganised as it has been, prolonged as it has been, and even, though fitfully, refreshed by some generous ideas, had this excellent effect? There are many who claim for it no less: but there are others who put a different question, and expect an answer of another sort.

Humanity, they say, is hard to come by, harder still to measure; men and women they know, as they meet them in the ordinary conditions of our modern life, maintaining themselves by their labour, earning a living by rendering definite services, as employed, to those who need definite services, as employers. Their question is, are the boys and girls sent out by the schools better able to render the services required or not? Humane they may be; they enquire, are they useful?

What are these services? Of the great majority of boys and girls who enter upon business careers, it would appear that the services required are to

begin with of a very simple and mechanical nature.
They call for patience, accuracy and, so far as it
can be combined with accuracy, speed. Although
in rendering these services the young employés have
opportunities of gathering experience of men and
things, and thus of quickening their intelligence and
strengthening their judgment, it is not their judgment and very little their intelligence which at the
outset their employers use. There always must be
in all occupations, whether of private or of commercial
and public life, an element of routine and mechanical
labour.

It is contended, and probably with some justice,
that work of this kind which can be done by a boy
of thirteen or fourteen will not be any better done by
a boy of sixteen or seventeen. It is even said that
it will be less well done by a boy who begins it at the
higher age, because he will quickly become impatient
of it. He will be conscious in himself of intelligence
and powers of judgment which his work does not
exercise; and he will be tempted to use his powers
prematurely: that is, before he is asked to use them,
and before he has had the experience upon which he
could use them with precision. If he does not feel
this temptation, or resists it, he will be accepting
himself, as his employer has already accepted him,
for a machine, and being uninterested in his work,
will feel a distaste for it, and thus become not a mere
machine but a discontented machine, and so slovenly.

But even if the boy of sixteen or seventeen does
the elementary routine work just as well as a boy

three or four years younger, a further difficulty arises: he will believe himself to be worth higher wages than those of the younger boy. His parents will support him in that opinion; they have maintained him and paid school fees for him for a prolonged period; or, even if his school fees and his maintenance have been provided from public funds, they will take into account that during these years, while other boys have been earning money, their boy has been earning none. If he is to begin at sixteen or seventeen upon wages no higher than those which are paid to younger boys, what compensation, they ask, do they get for what they call the sacrifices they have made on his behalf?

The employer seems to have an overwhelming reply: he is asking for a simple thing, and he is not prepared to pay a heavy price for it. The routine work has to be done. If the older boy can do it no better than the younger, he must not expect a higher wage. If, thanks to the generosity of his parents, or the benevolence of the State, his mind has been cultivated by several years of schooling more than his younger rivals have enjoyed, he must reckon that as a good thing, but he must not hope both to eat his cake and have it.

Yet this is exactly his desire, an illogical desire which we are all apt to cherish. What are the arguments by which it can be supported, and what are the devices by which it can be compassed? If it is admitted that elementary and mechanical work is the first to be done, it is said that the boy whose

schooling has been prolonged will reach perfection
in it more quickly than another who has not had his
advantages, and that he will be ready to emerge
from it more quickly to work of a higher kind in
which his better trained mind will find its scope.
Here two questions arise and claim an answer. The
first indeed we have already noticed; it is this: Is
it true, as a matter of fact, that the older boy does
reach perfection in the humbler tasks more quickly
than the younger boy? It is not every employer
who seems inclined to answer "Yes" to this question.
The second question is: Can it be reasonably maintained upon evidence that the boy who has had a
longer schooling possesses and exhibits superior
powers of judgment and initiative? There may be
a presumption in favour of this view, but evidence
is probably insufficient to support it, at any rate in
our own country.

The heads of great and successful businesses are
often men who have risen to the positions which
they hold from subordinate offices, and even in
many instances from the lowest offices in the concerns which they now control. Their training has
been practical; up to whatever age their school or
even their university education was carried, it came
sooner or later to an end, and they turned willingly
or regretfully to business. They are not quick to
admit that what they have learnt by the long and
unbroken discipline of business can be learnt more
rapidly or by different methods, and they are probably right in this; but it may be that great as is the

success which they have unquestionably attained they sometimes wonder whether there could be greater success of a different kind; that however is a problem for them to study by themselves in solitary reflection.

Every calling offers attractions to those who pursue it; it also imposes restrictions. A man who devotes himself to learning, philanthropy or religion rarely acquires great wealth; it may be that a man who devotes himself to the acquisition of wealth may miss some good things which those others secure. Humanity is an end which all men profess to seek, but it would appear that in seeking it they must accept the limitations of some particular calling, and so condemn themselves from the outset of their journey to reaching something short of their goal. There is indeed one mode of escape from this melancholy conclusion, a point of view in which these limitations can be transcended, but to that we shall come later.

The employer finds that in general the age of boys from whom he can recruit the lowest ranks in his service is higher now than it once was. He himself as a member of the State has joined with his fellow citizens in bringing about this change. He finds moreover that other employers, not many, perhaps, but yet some, take beginners into their service not at the lowest age which is now possible, but at an age somewhat in advance of that; and he and they turn to the schools with a very plausible demand. They say that the schools should prepare boys (better than they at present prepare them) for the work that they will have to do when they leave school.

The demand is plausible in appearance; it is sometimes made with reason, but not always. We have agreed that a part and perhaps a large part of the work of a beginner must be of a mechanical kind in which constant practice will produce perfection. If when it is claimed that the schools should prepare boys for their future work it is meant that the schools should send them out already drilled in this mechanical work, then the benefit which is supposed to be derived from continued schooling will be illusory. The boys will have been doing office work in school under unnatural and unreal conditions. They will not have been disciplined by the general training that the school is supposed to provide.

It may be further said on behalf of schools and schoolmasters, first that they cannot anticipate with anything approaching exactitude what occupations their pupils will follow when schooldays are over; and second, that even if they could forecast the future they could do little or nothing of the sort that is intended, for, after all, they are schoolmasters with such knowledge as they may possess of Latin or Greek or mathematics or natural science: they are not commercial men or heads of offices.

This plea will probably be allowed. Employers will either take boys into their firms at as early an age as the law permits, or if they take them two

or three years later they will take them without any
further definite preparation for the special work
which they will have to do; and upon the other side
the boys whose schooling has been prolonged, and
their parents and schoolmasters on their behalf,
must recognise that when they begin they must begin
at the beginning and get a beginner's wages.

There is another sense in which the schools may
seek to prepare boys for their work in life. They
may by their discipline and instruction make them
quick to learn, trustworthy in judgment and conduct,
ready in initiative, able to make and to keep pleasant
relations with their equals, and tolerant of authority.
It seems likely that in their own interests the heads of
businesses eagerly look out for such persons. It is
presumably worth their while to employ them and not
less worth their while to give them promotion. If,
therefore, employers say, as recently they have very
clearly said, that they look to the schools to prepare
boys for work, the schools cannot reply that the
employers are asking for anything which falls outside
the most generous definition of education.

But even when the demand of employers is made
with the reserve and the restraint which we have
attributed to them, it suggests a criticism upon the
schools, their methods and their results. And often,
as we know, the demand of the employers is more
trenchantly put, and the criticism not suggested but
made, that the schools are not, as adequately as they
might be, preparing boys for work, that they are
not training them as successfully as they might be

expected to train them in resourcefulness, initiative, judgment, loyalty and obedience.

The criticism is sometimes made uncharitably by foes; sometimes regretfully by friends; by the best schoolmasters, the shrewdest judges of their work, it is made, sometimes, with a disarming candour, of themselves. How far the best they achieve falls short of what they hope, only they can know. That they continue to hope, engaged as they are in a task to which success seems to be of necessity denied, pursuing a goal which ever recedes, is the measure of their fortitude. Scourged with the whips of practical men, they are beaten also with the scorpions of their own ideals. A famous scholar, delicately distinguishing the shades of colour given by Greek enclitics, and revealing also a certain amiable partiality, used to translate Τρῶες ῥα, "The Trojans, God help them!" Schoolmasters are Trojans, and need more than human succour.

What are they to do? Some, the most liberal of their critics, make the criticism we have just noted, and others clamour for a more technical and definite preparation for the duties of business life. They might meet both, by admitting what is the radical fault of our school system as by use and convention it has been fashioned. They might with truthful paradox say: The fault of our system is not that it is not technical and special enough; it is that it is already too technical and special.

The curriculum of our schools has been framed to meet the professional needs of clergy and schoolmasters. We have called this a radical fault in the curriculum; and yet perhaps we have not a right to use either word. The schools which have served as models for what are now called secondary schools, and have hitherto exercised not a solitary but a dominating influence on the programme of elementary schools, have been the grammar schools of the country, and these were set up to provide for the special needs of the classes which we have named. Into them, in the course of generations, the children of other classes have been drawn; children who, when they grew up, would inherit duties other than those which were peculiar and appropriate to these classes, and for whom the education offered by those schools in so far as it was specially appropriate to those classes, would be unsuitable as a preparation for the work which they on their part would have to do.

Milton no doubt speaks of a complete and liberal education as that which fits a man justly, skilfully and magnanimously to fulfil all the duties public or private, whether of peace or of war; and we may readily grant that a system of education which had these comprehensive results deserved to be called complete and liberal; but we may entertain a doubt whether the education provided by the grammar schools ever compassed these results, or was designed to compass them. Locke, at any rate, while ridiculing the claim that a farmer's son should learn Greek and Latin, is unwilling that the son of a gentleman should undergo the ordinary grammar school training.

For Locke, gentlemen form as distinct a class as farmers; they have an equally distinct and a different function, and it is by their function that the nature and the range of their education should, in his judgment, be determined. Gentlemen, he maintains, have special duties to perform in the State, and they must be prepared to perform them. Here is a plea for professional or technical education.

It is a plea which has been too little heeded. The ordinary education provided by the grammar schools came to be used more and more commonly by classes for whom it was not originally planned. This was very natural. To have done what Locke recommended, it would have been necessary to decide what a gentleman was, and then to construct and set in motion the machinery for educating him. Locke had for himself a tolerably clear notion both about the gentleman and about his schooling, but it is evident that his views were not generally held even in his own time: he wrote as a critic attacking the custom of his day. If the principle which underlies his theory of education had been accepted, special modes of education would have been conceded as necessary for other classes besides that with which he was himself mainly concerned. But the principle was not then conceded, and what it involves may not be fully understood even at the present time.

The idea of an education liberal and complete very properly touched the imagination of Englishmen, who are less practical than they like to think. Finding ready to their hands a system which was,

as we have seen, quite clearly professional and
technical, they tried to use it not only for its original
purpose, but as a general education. It is this
system, not of course unchanged, though surprisingly
little changed, which has survived to our own time.
It is curious to remark that it has served the general
even better than the professional purpose for which
it was instituted. Assailed as it is for its inadequacy
as a special preparation for those who hope to become
scholars, very commonly abandoned by those who
hope to become clergy, it is yet the education which
the rich Englishman provides for his sons out of
his ample resources, and which others, who can
ill afford it, provide from scanty funds for theirs,
because it has, or is reputed to have, a social value;
and since to a democracy nothing makes so potent
an appeal as social distinction, it, or something as
much like it as may be, is now provided for those
who cannot afford it at all, out of the public purse.

For everyone desires to be a gentleman, and if
he has some doubts about his own claim to the title,
he tries to support it by making sure that his son
shall be a gentleman. For our ancestors we cannot
answer; our children, if they cannot ennoble us,
may at any rate make us gentle.

It is very fit and proper that sacrifices should be
made for gentility, but a time comes when the
children must earn a living, and though to be a
gentleman is to render a service to society, and
perhaps the greatest of services, it is not in itself
a source of income. This simple fact is the origin

of the present demand for commercial and other
kinds of special education. Are we then to give
up gentility and general education, and devise a
"practical" education which will lead our children
straight and fast to employment decently, and
perhaps handsomely, paid? Or shall we cultivate
gentility and encourage general education, hoping
that other things such as men are apt to covet,
a livelihood among the rest, will be added? Is this
too sanguine an optimism? Shall we not try to
make a judicious compromise, and allow a general
education up to a certain point, and insist on professional and technical studies afterwards? A compromise is never judicious. It is not a golden mean ;
the golden mean is, as Aristotle claimed, an extreme.
It is a high ridge, difficult, it is true, for travelling,
but the line along which convergent heights run and
reach their loftiest level. To move along it one
must sacrifice much, but never a principle.

It is too easily assumed that education, and
specially liberal education, is the gift of schools and
colleges and to be had from them only. They can
do much, but they cannot do everything, and it is
to treat not merely "business" but the world un-
fairly, to deny them any share in the work of liberal
education. On the other hand we have to recognise
that to pursue any "subject" or to follow any profession far is to abandon other subjects, to renounce
other professions. And it would seem that the
general cultivation of the mind must yield to the
claims of special callings. A man who is engaged

in teaching sacrifices some of his opportunities for
research, even in the subject which he teaches.   He
might know more of his subject if he taught it less.

But a man's opportunities of general education
are limited not only by the exigencies of his calling.
Indeed, the word "general" has led to some confusion
of thought and to some blinking of facts.   When we
say that a child is offered a general education, we
use the phrase in two senses which should be distinguished.   We think of him first as an imperfectly
developed creature.   In the process of development
"the indefinite and homogeneous precedes the
definite and heterogeneous.   The first germ of the
organism is a uniform mass, in which no definite
structure can be distinguished[1]."   Just as the
development of societies is marked by the distinction
of classes and of functions and by the division of
labour, so it is with the individual.   A child, when
born, has already got some such distinction of
structure and of function, but very little as compared
with an adult man.   Compared with a man, he is
indefinite and homogeneous.   His education, like
everything else that he receives at all, he receives
as a whole with the whole of himself: it is general
for him.   But we use the word also in another way,
when we intend to describe an education which is
of wide scope, in which many subjects are included.

Now we offer children a general education in the
second sense partly because we know that they are
themselves in an undeveloped, or "general" condition,

---

[1] Höffding, *Psychology*, p. 90.

in which all is "grist that comes to the mill" (trusting the mill to forbid the approach of what is not grist) ; and partly because we know so little about them, and can conjecture very dimly what special aptitudes they will presently develop. Sooner or later, more or less decisively, some special aptitudes reveal themselves, partly by their eminence and strength, and partly as survivals; in other respects and for other things, we have to admit they have no aptitude, and we arrive at their positive powers by what the logicians call the method of elimination.

To put the case in another, perhaps a more distressful, but a more convincing way: all of us, sooner or later, reach our "saturation point" in regard to many matters; we have taken in as much of them as we can take in; we can take in no more. We continue to receive only such things as we have capacity for, and if these are fewer than we could wish, our interest in them is keener than the diffused and vague or "general" interest which we previously felt in a much larger number of things. And, though the things which we can now assimilate to ourselves are less numerous than of old, of these things the total amount that we can accept is greater than the former total which was made up of many and various elements.

The dangers that attend specialised education are apparent, and the chief are two: first, it may fail to provide something necessary to the general well-being of the pupil, something the lack of which will make him less human and humane than he might,

with it, have become; second, it may assail him with
a subject (or subjects) which he is quite incapable of
accepting, or which his general training has been
insufficient to enable him properly and proportion-
ately to use.

Oddly enough, the dangers of general education
can be described in almost the same language; the
chief are, again, two: first, it may offer to the pupil
and press upon his acceptance a number of subjects,
many or most of which he cannot accept, subjects
which in fact for him are not the means and the
material for general development, subjects, mechanical and enforced occupation with which wastes his
time and blunts his intelligence; second, it may
fail to provide him, or may provide him very imperfectly, with the one or two subjects which he
can now accept, assimilate, and use as the means,
the material for the particular development appropriate to his nature at its present stage.

A perfect education would be one which offered
a never-ending general development as a basis for
an infinite variety of special excellences. It is not
to blame our schools and Universities to say that such
an education they do not supply. We are content
with something less than that. We are content
with a *certain amount* of general development, and
a *certain amount* of special power. If the precise
point at which general education should give place
to special education could be determined, it would
have to be determined for each individual, and
education would become a sort of therapeutics, with

prescriptions made for every individual person upon a separate diagnosis. But education is not that, and we may be thankful that it is not that. A higher precision than we have yet achieved is, of course, to be desired for the appropriate education of the individual; but an education which was designed exclusively for the individual would abandon its main virtue, which is its social quality. The business of the educator is far more to build up a society, a nation, than to elaborate a hygiene for the individual. A society is not made of all-round, perfectly developed people any more than a pavement or a house is made of circular bricks. It is the imperfections as much as the virtues of people which make them fit together in the social edifice. If the "fitting" is at present ill-conceived and ill-adjusted, we shall not improve matters by attempting to produce people who could not possibly, because of their very rounded perfections, fit together.

Gain brings loss; whatever a man does he does at the sacrifice of other things which he might do, but in fact sets aside; in proportion to his ability is his disability. We pay not only for what we get, but for what we are, and enter into life, hardly if at all, and even so, mutilated and maimed, shorn of the glittering hopes of inchoate youth, pruned to the quick by the sharp knife of necessity. We may well be content if indeed, for all our manifest shortcomings, it is life into which we enter. Upon one condition is the entrance made, and it is a condition too little remembered by those who speak of

commercial education.   Renunciation is the price of
life, the self-imposed self-surrender of the individual
for the sake of the community.

A society, a nation, is a larger whole, a more
spiritual unity, than the individual men and women
who are reckoned its members; if they are to
apprehend its reality at all, it must be by an effort
of the imagination.   But—it is necessary to remember—a society, a nation, is also larger than the
groups of people into which it may be divided;
these groups have their justification so far only as
they are truly parts of it, contributing jointly to
its total strength and goodness[1].   Else they are

[1] Cp. H. G. Wells, *The Passionate Friends*, p. 237:
"I have long since ceased to trouble about the economics of
human society.   Ours are not economic but psychological diffi-
culties.   There is enough for everyone, and only a fool can be
found to deny it.   But our methods of getting and making are
still ruled by legal and social traditions from the time before we
had tapped these new sources of power, before there was more
than enough for everyone, and when a bare supply was only
secured by jealous possession and unremitting toil.   We have
no longer to secure enough by a stern insistence.   We have come
to a plenty.   The problem now is to make that plenty go round,
and *keep it enough* while we do.

Our real perplexities are altogether psychological.   There are
no valid arguments against a great-spirited Socialism but this,
that people will not.   Indolence, greed, meanness of spirit, the
aggressiveness of authority, and above all jealousy, jealousy for
our pride and vanity, jealousy for what we esteem our possessions,
jealousy for those upon whom we have set the heavy fetters of
our love, a jealousy of criticism and association, these are the
real obstacles to those brave, large reconstructions, those profitable abnegations and brotherly feats of generosity that will yet
turn human life—of which our individual lives are but the

organised enemies both of the individual and of
society, incorporated selfishnesses which exact from
individuals what is due only to the community as
a whole, and cut the sinews of society. We are
emerging from the primitive state in which man
fought against his neighbour for a living with the
rough weapons of savagery; we have not yet
emerged from a state in which groups of men, led
by an enterprising and able chief, make with more
elaborate weapons a deadlier warfare upon rival
groups; but we may well believe that the imagination by which the group was called into existence,
may call into a more vivid existence a real society
which will transcend the group. Just as family-
feeling may be either a national asset or a national
danger, in proportion to its collective unselfishness
or its collective selfishness, so and in like proportion
commercial alliances, "businesses," may be a national
asset or a national danger. As the head of a family
should encourage family-feeling and foster it in the
hope that the generous sentiments sheltered at first
within that narrow boundary may escape and spread
beyond it; as he should certainly refuse to gather
to himself, and hug, a devotion which touches the
highest level of loyalty when the person to whom it
is offered becomes, in a royal sense, representative;—
so the head of a business must not ask for himself or
for his firm a sacrifice rightly due to society at large,

momentary parts—into a glad, beautiful and triumphant co-
operation all round this sunlit world.

If but humanity could have its imagination touched...."

a sacrifice to be paid to himself or his firm only if and so far as they represent society.

A school has a double relation towards society: it is the servant of society and must do what it is told; but it is part of society and must help to frame the demand. And more than this, schoolmasters and other teachers are human creatures, responsible of course to society, but responsible to themselves also. Their duty to themselves does not indeed counter their duty to society in the largest and most liberal meaning; but it may conflict with the claims made upon them by that special section or group of the total society, their Governors, their Committees, or the employers of their pupils when they leave the teachers' hands. Occasion for dramatic heroism is not to be sought: we need not picture to a distressed imagination a multitude of silent suffering school-masters, nobly starving because they will not lower their standards or demean a great profession. But a clear understanding the teachers should have with those who, as functions have come to be distributed, have a certain influence and control over them. The teachers should ask certain questions and press for an answer. They should ask their employers, the employers of their pupils: "What is it, after all, that you want? What are the qualities that you desire to find in young persons who seek positions in your firms? And by what age do you expect these qualities to have been developed? And again, what of qualifications as they may be distinguished from qualities? What kinds of knowledge and skill

do you require, and once more at what age?" These
are fair questions to be asked and answered. If
they were boldly asked and openly answered much
good would be wrought, much evil would be done
away. Some employers, tacitly but in effect, are
asking for living machines. Will they openly ask
for living machines? Then there will be some
schoolmasters ready to reply, not less openly, that
their work, as schoolmasters, is not to produce living
machines, but live intelligence.

But these questions, openly asked, will provoke
answers not only open but generous. That mechanical work has to be done—not only by those who
hold the lowest, but by those who hold the highest
positions—may be agreed. Schoolmasters at any
rate are not likely to deny it: the head of a school
has more, not less, mechanical work to do than his
youngest assistant. But the mechanical work is to
be done by people who are not to be made themselves
mechanical either in order to do it or in process of
doing it: it is to be done by people who will illumi-
nate it with intelligence and use its details as the
materials for the constructive imagination.

"Life," wrote Samuel Butler in one of his *Note-
Books*, "is the art of drawing sufficient conclusions
from indifferent premises." In letters, in science, in
commerce, in statesmanship, success is won by those
who can draw conclusions. The premises are never
sufficient; it is not merely in number that they fall
short, but in kind. It is not prudent to draw conclusions without premises, the most numerous and

the most suggestive that can be got; but it is folly
to wait till the conclusion is forced upon a hesitant
mind; such a conclusion, if it comes at all, is an end,
a termination. The conclusion to which a man leaps
(always in a twilight, if not in the dark) is a point
of departure as much as a point of arrival. Seeing
a chance, seizing an opportunity, putting two and
two together and making a total greater than a
dull addition would warrant,—these are said to
be characteristic performances of the good man of
business.

When Aristotle claimed that virtue was a
"mean," he was careful to show that the "mean"
is not discovered by a merely arithmetical calcula-
tion. It is not absolute, but relative to the persons
concerned and to the occasion; the "mean" in fact
is the right thing for the time, the place and the
persons in question; and that is why it is an "extreme." And virtue, he says, reaches its mark,
hits the "mean," by *making shots*.

A liberal and a commercial education will train
the courage for leaping to conclusions, will quicken
the mind for this happy divination of what is appropriate.

CHAPTER III

STANDARDS IN TASTE AND MORALS[1]

Let us take in order the words which make up the title—Standard—Taste—Morals—and set down upon each some statements which have won or may win general agreement, and then arrange the several conclusions to which these statements seem to point, and lastly compare the conclusions one with another.

"A standard," according to the *Encyclopaedia Britannica*, is a "fixed weight, measure, value or quality established by law or customarily recognised as a unit of comparison by which the correctness of others can be determined....The use of the term for a recognised unit of comparison is due probably to the fact that it is something fixed or set up, stable; and not to any fanciful reference to the ensign or flag as the object to which one turns as a rallying point."

A standard, evidently, must be easily recognised and without dispute or hesitation accepted if it is to deserve its name. But to say so much as this is at once to raise several interesting and difficult questions. By whom, we may ask, is the standard to be recognised? and for what purpose is it to be used? Let us recall for a moment the alternative words given

[1] Reprinted, with permission, from the *Proceedings of the Liverpool Literary and Philosophical Society.*

by the *Encyclopaedia Britannica* for standard—not less than four are given, and more might quite easily have been given. Weight is subject to standard, but a standard by weight is of no use to a man who desires to reckon distance or size; measure, a somewhat ambiguous word, generally indicates spatial dimension, but a measure of this sort is of no use to a man whose concern is with weight; value, once more an ambiguous word, we may take as indicating the preciousness, or as we more commonly put it, the price of things; but the preciousness of gold as compared with that of silver or of copper, cannot be judged either by weight or by measured size. Quality, a more general word still, is used most frequently when we give our regard to the constituent elements of things which may perhaps be weighed, measured and priced, but which we choose to consider in another light—so we speak of the quality of some fabric, the quality of a wine, or the quality of an action, or of *quality* simply, and without as yet determining how it is to be exhibited, in what material or in what action, without indeed surmising whether it is to be exhibited at all,—so richness may be ascribed to a fabric but also to a voice, mellowness to a wine or to a stained glass window or to old age, and we may speak of mercy, truth and justice without ascribing them to any person or looking for their embodiment in any act.

A standard used for one purpose will not serve another purpose; there are different standards in different fields of human conduct and interest.

But let us turn to the other question—by whom is it to be recognised? It is well recognised by persons whose occupation is wholly or mainly in one or other of these several fields, and less easily by others, and not at all by persons who have no concern whatever in these regions. "Weight" and "measure," recognised most readily by persons who constantly have occasion to measure and to weigh, are recognised, of course, though less easily, by other persons; but those weights and measures are recognised which a man uses in dealing with things with which he is familiar—a carpenter for instance recognises a foot and a footrule, but he might well be at a loss if he heard the word "hand" used as a˙measure, though a man who trafficked in horses would be in no difficulty at all: and a coal merchant might confess himself unfamiliar with the names of weights endeared by familiarity to a chemist. About "values" there is less agreement. The value, for instance, of a house is differently estimated by several men who contemplate purchasing it, and if all of them should agree in differing from the man who desires to sell it, we should be confronted with no unusual, though a troublesome, phenomenon. This is the more remarkable, because *value* has a wider range of meaning than *weight* or even than *measure*. Where, it would appear, men ought most easily to be agreed they are most sharply divided. We may, for a moment longer, pursue this line of investigation, and look again at the word *quality*. The quality of a sound, the quality of a colour are very variously apprehended and diversely expressed by critics who need not count lack of confidence among their shortcomings; and there may of course be critics of a finer temper who are less sure of themselves, who apprehend sometimes in one fashion sometimes in another, vividly now, less vividly at another moment, or if not less vividly yet with varying perception, and whose words for what they perceive vary too. Justice is a quality, and mercy a quality; but if we are to temper justice with mercy, what is the result? Is it something less than justice, other than mercy? Whatever our conclusion may be we cannot state it in the form of an addition sum—so much justice plus so much mercy; and however we state it, our words will not avail perfectly to assure our neighbours that our thoughts are their thoughts.

We appear, then, to be forced to this position: we must allow that the same standards are not applicable in different departments of life and speculation; and that within the same departments the meaning of standards varies in the use of persons who are speaking about the same subject, and who are making a serious effort to be exact and to reach agreement.

Moreover we expressly and deliberately vary the meaning of our words, even when we use them in connexion with the same standards and in the same general field, but about different objects in it. The word *tall* for instance conveys the notion of height, measured, let us say, in feet and inches; but we do not convey the same notion when we speak of a tall

man as when we speak of a tall tree or of a tall hat;
and we intend something different once more when
we characterise a story as tall.   We may with equal
security but with different intention, speak of a
mountain and the price of coal as being high, and
we may call ourselves and our neighbours to admire
the height of devotion or of folly which a man may
reach.

At once the objection will be raised that we are
passing from the ordinary to a metaphorical use of
words: my purpose has been to raise it, and I shall
later attempt a reply to it.   In the meanwhile I shall
say without apology or argument that when we
declare that a man is tall and presently that his son,
a boy of 12, is tall, though we may measure both
with the same measure against the same door, we
are not using the same standard for the two—there
is one standard for a man, another for a child.

This homely observation may offer us an entrance
to a problem as attractive as it is perplexing.   If we
return to the *Encyclopaedia*, we see again that a
standard is "established by law or customarily
recognised."   It is, then, founded on convention,
based on agreement, protected by legal enactment
or sanctioned by use and wont.   But a convention
has a date, an agreement is made at some point of
time, and if not our knowledge, at least, our imagination can travel back to it, and we may ask, what of
our standard before that momentous hour?   Or will
our inquiry be hushed by the discreet reminder that
the standard was but born in that very hour; or

shall we be told more plainly that we have mis-
understood the whole problem, and that standard,
convention and agreement are but three names for
one and the same thing?   We can at any rate make
a plausible case against the accusation, and give
good reason for pursuing what seemed for an instant
to be a temerarious and even an improper inquiry.

Let us take the first of these alternatives.   If a
convention is established by law, then law must have
preceded convention—preceded, that is to say, any
particular convention in which we may happen to be
interested, and for the origin and support of which
we look to law,—but what are we to say of law itself?
Is law itself a convention or not?   Sir George
Cornewall Lewis in his work, *The Use and Abuse of
Political Ideas*, a treasury of exact thought, ordered
learning and precise statement, declares (following
Blackstone) that "law excludes the idea of compact;
for a compact is a promise proceeding *from* us, law
is a command directed *to* us.   The language of compact is 'I will or will not, do this'; that of a law is
'Thou shalt or shalt not, do it.'   No agreement can
exist, except in a moral sense, between a sovereign
and his subjects, between a government and people,
as there is no legitimate means of enforcing it."
It would appear from this that a convention, an
agreement or a bargain is somehow made, and that
law enforces the strict observance of it.   The parties
to the convention are subject to the law, without
which the convention could not be maintained
since either party, or both might break it with

impunity. Again, Sir George Lewis writes:—"The only proper mode of determining a dispute as to the existence or construction of a law, is by application to a competent tribunal, which alone has authority to decide it." And he adds immediately, "Law, however, is often used to denote, not the commands of a sovereign, but certain moral rules, the existence of which can only be determined by the arguments of private individuals, and not by the authority of public officers. It is in this sense that we speak of the law of God, the law of nature, the laws of honour, etc."

What then, is this tribunal which can decide a dispute not only as to the "construction" but even as to the "existence" of a law? Is it the embodiment of law; or are we to say that it has been created by law, or on the contrary that law derives from it?

We may remind ourselves that to whatever objections the theory lies open which finds the origin of Society in a compact or contract, the theory has profoundly affected both political and social theory and practice, and does afford, if not an historical account of the beginnings of Society, at any rate a very valuable and cogent logical account of the powers and operations of Society when from whatever origin, it has sprung into being. The truth is, we cannot attach any meaning to the word law until we have postulated Society, nor to Society until we have presumed the existence of a Sovereign. The Sovereign may be a monarch, or a Committee

or a Democracy; but in whatever form sovereignty
shows itself, it yields obedience to none, it claims
and receives obedience from the community which it
governs, and which, without that governance, could
not exist. "The sovereign"—I quote once more and
for the last time from Lewis—"has the complete
disposal of the life, rights and duties of every member
of the community. It has also power to modify or
change the existing form of government. There is
no law which it has not power to alter, repeal or
enact." Who is this sovereign? And we must
press an even shrewder inquiry: "How is it that
those very matters escape his decision and control
in which the greatest variations are possible, in
which the curtailment or restriction of variations
most grievously impedes human progress—just as
their unchecked development may produce the
greatest misfortunes—how is it, in a word, that his
powers end where the interests of men assume their
keenest vivacity?" "The Law of God, the laws of
nature, the laws of honour," claim another origin
and a different sanction. "The words lawful and
unlawful," wrote Archbishop Whately, "are sometimes employed with reference to the law of the land
and sometimes to the law of God and the dictates
of a sound conscience; so that the same thing may
be lawful in one sense, which is unlawful in
another."

The Archbishop was, no doubt, able to recall a
sentence from the Book of Proverbs—"Divers
measures are an abomination to the Lord," and his

experience of the world must have taught him that
they cause infinite confusion among men.

Gathering up the considerations and questions
which have suggested themselves, we may now
perhaps say: that a standard ought to be clearly
seen and understood, it ought to be general or even
universal in its application, conformity to it being
enforced, and dissent in some fashion penalised: it
is set up by a sovereign; but we have also to add
that in fact a standard recognised and respected by
some men fails to win the recognition and hold the
respect of others, that a standard valid in one department of human inquiry or preoccupation may not
be valid in another; that while a standard may be
a convention binding upon men in that region which
we call legal, it is not upheld by the same sanction
in that larger region which we call moral, that the
same or similar penalties do not attend its neglect
or violation in both domains; and finally that of the
nature and origin of the sovereign who establishes
and maintains the standard, very little, if anything,
can be said, except in the terms of law, from which
convention draws its strength, or of a tribunal which
in turn interprets law or asserts its existence and
defines its range; and such a tribunal must either
represent the sovereign or actually be the sovereign.
And this may well be condemned as a very unsatisfactory result to reach after so vexatious an
investigation.

Perhaps we shall meet with a better reward for
a further search, and we can make it in simpler

language. The practical, everyday answers to the questions "Why am I to do this?" and "Why is this right or that wrong?" are "Because most other people, or all other people, do this," and "Because I have always heard that this is right and that is wrong," and a man who should invariably press behind these usual, these conventional replies would spend all his life in raising questions which the world would not stay to answer, and could not answer if it stayed. For clearly a man who is not content with what satisfies his neighbours, desires something personal and peculiar to himself, and this he must get for himself, for his neighbours will not supply it, not simply from lack of goodwill or interest, but from lack of ability. If he finds unsuitable for himself the ordinary houses in which ordinary folk live placidly and even thankfully, he must build for himself, and even so must ask the aid of other men who will not perfectly understand or execute his designs; he must avail himself of timber, bricks or stones, the very materials out of which the children of convention make habitations comfortable to themselves if painful to his special taste; even if he climbs a tree and makes his simple abode there, he must choose a tree from among those which nature has provided, and he will complain idly of the inconveniences which in the speech of the vulgar are associated with that kind of dwelling place: he may find it hard to keep his balance at the height to which his fastidious imagination has urged him; he may find it even harder to come down. And yet what ignominy to beg the assistance of the despised multitude to rescue you from your solitary eminence! Prudence and indolence alike counsel us to do what other men do, and to accept as right what is commonly so regarded.

But upon a man the most respectable and ordinary, once perhaps in a lifetime of inconspicuous resemblance to his fellows, there comes, like a sudden wind breaking the far-stretched equability of a level sky, a passion to be himself, a lust for difference and distinction, that cannot be resisted or gainsaid. Like a wind it bears him, uncontrolled except by its own vehemence, unquestioning, passive and obedient to its enthralling mastery, to some splendid extravagance, to some gorgeous imbecility; he wears a frock coat and the garments which befit and accompany it, all of them except boots; barefoot he goes, but dauntless, his delicate feet warmed and protected by the shining transparency of his idealism. Or, an individual once more, and bursting the soft fetters of the usual and the safe, the imperious victim of a more imperious impulse, he incontinently sells all that he possesses and gives to the poor. He does not ask in those rare moments of mad or saintly illumination what the world thinks, he neither seeks approval nor shuns censure; indifferent to both, he does what he likes and declares that it is good, and pays to enthusiasm the homage customarily rendered to law. Passion has wrested the sceptre from convention; freedom has taken the seat of ousted and outraged authority. And we look on with little

either of pity or of vexation in our hearts, and use
the strange words of a paradox which much repetition
on the lips of men has worn to smoothness. "He
will come to his senses," we say; and "he will come
to himself," meaning that he will return to the
common fashion of dress or of charity. And in
most cases we are right enough: the gust which
seized the object of our very temperate commisera-
tion dies as suddenly as it was born; the mood of
eccentric self-sacrifice quickly passes; and he who
took our wonder for a moment is restored, booted
like ourselves, and swayed by emotions no more
violent than our own. Or if not, the world, richly
provided with hospitals for sick minds, will commit
him to a seclusion in which he will not affront our
sense of propriety by an unduly prolonged exhibition
of singularity; or else, should he prove intractable
and menacing, will drive him out into the wilderness
which is the only home for the irreconcileable and
the absurd. Then we may trust our large powers of
forgetfulness to blot or erase a disconcerting picture.
Out of his mind we call him, and for punishment we
attempt, with rarely broken success, to put him out
of our minds as well. Broken rarely, the success with
which we rebuild our tranquillity, is yet broken sometimes. A chivalrous act, a supreme penance self-
imposed and endured with the smile either of irony
or of untroubled composure, a great sentence, once
uttered and not to be silenced by the gross sounds
of prosperous wisdom, the unworldly precept
launched upon a cautious world to take no thought

for the morrow, the conflicting but coequal doctrines, one, that the kingdom of heaven suffers violence, the other, that it is only to be entered by little children—these astonishing deeds and words make their unerring course, like arrows barbed in heaven and divinely poisoned, to the hearts of men, and fix themselves there; like some music, which turns to discord what we had earlier greeted, and still strive to keep, as harmonies, they pierce the mind with beauty, and arraign our very judgment; they beat like the unwearying sea upon a bastioned shore, and shake the foundations of our solid world. Unconquered and yet unconquering, or at best moving very slowly to contested triumph, they shine like a light in the darkness, uncomprehended but inextinguishable. Shall we deny that these are standards? And yet can we pretend that they are by law established, or by custom recognised?

Rather with law and custom they seem to wage a truceless war, receiving from their natural enemies the tribute of mockery or of contradiction. They cannot be brought as subjects within the pale of use, but no more can they be banished or ignored: exceptional, they will not take, even when it is offered to them, the rank of the merely pre-eminent and the distinguished, for they silently assert their difference of quality. If men should argue "This, after all, is charity, and this courage, and this is but one other of our own familiar virtues raised to a higher level than the ordinary, more nobly proportioned and richly endowed"—they but veil under these words

a flattery offered to themselves, and show that they
have not perceived the transcendent quality of the
things they seek by such measures to appraise.   It
is to the credit of human honesty and intelligence
that they seldom argue so; they leave the heroic in
isolation, admitting its difference, and attempting
to withhold their allegiance; and follow their
accustomed orbit.

They are modest men, they say; they keep well
within the bounds marked for them by their fathers
and observed by their contemporaries; they claim
no more for themselves than those others, men of
repute, were fain to hold.

It would, they go on, in complacent self-defence,
be not indeed a failure, but an error of taste to do
otherwise.   Taste, the most individual and incom-
municable of judgments, is for them a judgment
common and certain; they are not at a loss to
determine what is taste, good taste; it is the taste
of the people with whom they consort, and it is
exhibited in the things which these persons approve.
Rotund in mind they very naturally argue in a circle;
these things, they say, are allowed and enjoined by
good taste, and good taste consists in these things.
How perfect a standard to which all things conform;
how perfect a world governed by so admirable and
efficient a canon!

What is a canon?   Let us make appeal again to
the *Encyclopaedia*, where we shall find a most
interesting paragraph.   "The Greek word...means
originally a straight rod or pole, and metaphorically

what serves to keep a thing upright or straight,
a rule.   In the New Testament it occurs in Gal. vi. 16,
and 2 Cor. x. 13, 15, 16—signifying in the former
passage a measure, in the latter what is measured
a district." It is to be noted, what the writer of
the article does not deem it necessary to remark, that
the *rule* transcends and by an undreamt fulfilment,
abolishes hitherto accepted rules, and that the
district or province is wider than any hitherto
delimited.   But let us not interrupt him longer;
he continues "the two general applications of the
word fall mainly into two groups, in one of which the
underlying meaning is that of rule, in the other that
of a list or catalogue, *i.e.*, of books containing the
rule."

The two meanings are exactly comparable to
those which we have given to the word taste, and
the distinction between the two just what we have
already drawn.

But we must follow our inquiry yet further.   In
Wilson's *Rhetoric*, written in 1553, and quoted by
Sir James Murray in the *New English Dictionary* we
may read a definition of canon and canonical:
"Such as all the world hath confirmed and agreed
upon, that (it) is authentic and canonical." But
here we come back to an earlier and a recurrent
problem, why has all the world "confirmed and
agreed upon" this and not upon that, upon these
ways of action and of thought rather than upon
others?   How is the canon established? and why?
But to ask these questions is to criticise the criterion,

and if we have the audacity to do that once we may
do it twice, and endlessly, for ever seeking more
remote tests for receding standards; or is there some
limit to this process?   If we accept what is confirmed
and agreed upon, we may very easily be misled.
"Wisdom under a ragged coat," says Crosse in
Virtue's Commonwealth, "is seldom canonical."

The proper object of dutiful regard, it would seem,
may be disregarded or treated with hostility or con-
tempt, for want of a livery.   Are we then to strip all
the ideas and actions which we encounter, to avoid
the risk of confounding friends and foes?   Or is it
wisdom's duty to wear a good coat, of the usual stuff
and cut to the fashion, for its own safety and our
convenience?   And for our own conduct are we to
halt for ever in hesitant self-examination?   Is it
not possible for us to do what clearly it would be
convenient for us to do, namely to have recourse at
once to a standard, accessible, unmistakable, definite
and final?   In Holland's *Pliny* we have an instructive
sentence: "Moreover he hath made that which work-
men call canon, that is to say, one absolute piece of
work, from whence artificers do fetch their draughts,
symmetries and proportions."   An excellent practice
for artificers; "theirs not to reason why," theirs but
to take instructions and copy models and work to
a design made by other hands.   For artificers a
tolerable and, indeed, an excellent arrangement; but
for artists, no, and therefore for human beings, no,
since art is their inalienable prerogative.   Not less
certainly and far more vehemently than men crave

the comforting warmth, the supporting pressure of
the crowd, they long for space and air; they want
independence without loneliness, and company without constraint. The absolute piece of work fashioned
to express the ideas and hopes of another mind they
cannot always accept as the model for the fresh
incarnation of their own ideas. When—and that is
for the most part their condition—they are unvisited
by ideas, they can express conventions in conventional forms; but let ideas break their calm, and the
model serves no more. What is to guide them on
the way from tradition, through discontent, to progress? Example, fortified by age-long reverence, has
suddenly lost its potency. They envy the liberty of
the enthusiast and the eccentric because they have
guessed his secret; he is impelled by a purpose
greater than himself, he revolves upon a circle
larger than their own, he is unassailable because
the vassal of an unseen power, the bondsman of
authority. But if convention, the summary and
epitome of things ordinarily admired, cannot exercise
because it does not possess this authority, no more
can mere spontaneity make a law for itself. The
hat or waistcoat in which youth pays its touching
homage to the idea of elegance may seize our attention, and exercise our patience, but it cannot always
win our assent; for though formality may be the
inglorious badge of maturity, and a certain rigidity
may be the regretted though pardoned token of old
age, we shall still mark off effrontery from freedom,
and note the contrast between disciplined ease and

exuberant licence. But what must be our judgment if we saw in a dress or a house, in a picture or a poem, a vision of beauty strange to our eyes and yet compelling and convincing? By no precedent has that artist been guided; no model or example or pattern has moulded him; his appeal is to Authority, and we not only see what he has wrought, but catch a glimpse at least of the power to which he has abandoned himself, a power which snatches our allegiance, and, if but a moment, retains it.

Whenever such fortune befalls us, whenever our eyes and minds are filled by such a sight, we instantly break down the barriers which divide one part from another of our appreciation and of our life. "True taste," wrote Ruskin in *A Joy For Ever*, "or the instantaneous preference of the noble thing to the ignoble, is a necessary accompaniment of high worthiness in nations or men." But he wrote in language more apt because less cautious in the *Crown of Wild Olive*, "Taste is not only a part and an index of morality;—it is the only morality." If then we could track Authority to its seat and source in the domain of Taste, we should have found it also in Morality.

For what, we must now ask, is Morality? We might, of course, answer, and without fear of contradiction, that morality means the sum of acts approved by men as conforming to a code or a type also approved; and we might say that custom has lent approval to certain acts and to a certain code or codes, and withheld it from others. All this may

be true, but it is not enough; we must find the source
of action and the ground of approbation. We find
both in human will. The will of man, directed by
his intellect and urged by his desire, but surpassing
both in range and power, pursues an ideal in which
he may find himself, with which he may identify
himself. The long, the endless road towards this ideal
is marked by many stages travelled, step by step.
Every act and thought of a man makes such a step.
But it is made not merely as a step, or a stage
towards a distant goal; in each step as he goes he
must realise himself; in each finite achievement
he must see the imprint and note the signature of
the infinite; in each, the end must in a sense and
in a measure be already attained; but yet in each
the comparison is drawn, the strong contrast felt,
between so much of the ideal as has been won and
the ideal itself in its fulness and completeness. For
progress is measured on the one hand by the distance
travelled from the starting point, and on the other
by the space which yet separates us from our goal.

Progress is essential to our notion of an ideal.
Here we meet an old problem—for if we grant this
are we not setting the goal of all effort at an immeasurable distance? If progress is for ever to be
maintained, can the end ever be reached? Can an
end reached be an ideal, of which progress is an
essential quality? And once more how between an
infinitely remote beginning and an infinitely remote
destination can progress be marked as we have
claimed that it must be and that it is?

The best answer in prose I know to this difficult question is that of T. H. Green, made in language itself necessarily difficult.

"Moral goodness is devotion to a moral ideal, which we regard as a divine principle of improvement in man. But this progress and development cannot be a mere process to infinity; it must have an end in an eternal state of being, in which self-conscious personality is maintained; and since the realisation of human personality can mean nothing except its realisation in society, then for all the differences of function between different members of society, it must imply in all of them the fulfilment of the idea of humanity, *i.e.*, devotion to the perfection of man. The moral ideal, then, has at once a personal and a social character."

This doctrine is familiar in poetic writing. Whenever a man reaches any pure height of personal achievement in thought or action, he is aware of sympathies and connexions with other men and with the world at large of which he was ignorant at a lower level: being more truly than at other times himself, he is more than himself; or as we may express the same fact in other words, a man is only one with himself when he is at one with the world. The inner harmony is not indeed accompanied by an outer, larger harmony; rather, the inner harmony is taken up into and becomes a general and universal concord. We know quite well what is meant when we are told that a vast number of people, for all the variety and divergence of their several interests, occupations and origins, rise or move as "one man." For an instant, if for no more, they are drawn into a unity, they are no longer a mere crowd or concourse of men and women; they are more than an association or a party; they are one spirit, one soul. Religious writers, who have most need for poetic expression, being most concerned with poetry, that creative, vitalising and simplifying passion, have from age to age used this singular language without question or challenge. The Church itself, spreading through all lands, numbering its members in all ages of the past, including in its timeless and spaceless bounds the dead and the yet unborn, is called a bride: a bride adorned, not with the spangled decorations of incongruous virtues, but with a beauty consistent with her own nature, at each stage of its ripening development, and prophetic already of her final ineffable splendour. And yet again, and as we perceive quite naturally, the figure changes, and the amazing allegory offers to our eyes a city, four square, shining with the confluent lights of many jewels, peopled but unified—a city, but a person still, holding in its infinite simplicity the manifold qualities of ten thousand times ten thousand spirits, a commonwealth, but a single soul. One with themselves, their fellow-citizens, and their spiritual habitation, they have that very perfection which we call artistic, for the mode of their being is identical with being itself; since the just and ultimate expression of an idea is the idea itself fulfilled and made manifest. But the doctrine of the philosophers receives a yet more astonishing illustration or proof (for illustration, when light directed upon any object of visual regard oi inner speculation meets and merges in the light which shines from within, becomes proof). Such a city is the far and final resting-place of men; reached by long pilgrimage of the feet, it is built by laborious hands; its inhabitants have made it by travelling towards it; there they repose after toil, and dwell in undisturbed, unthreatened security; but more conspicuous than its other constellated glories, the very thread which holds its matched and ordered jewels, is a road,—"a high-road shall be there and a way." Hope continues though per-fection is won, progress is maintained in established peace.

"Human excellence by no means depends upon the greater sum of *single, rigorously moral*, actions, but upon the greater congruence of the whole native disposition with the moral law; and it is a small recommendation to an age or a people, if we hear much among them concerning morality and single moral deeds; rather may we hope that in the climax of culture, if such a thing can be imagined, there will be little *talk* about it[1]."

[1] Schiller.—"Upon the Moral Use of Aesthetic Manners" (*Philosophical and Aesthetic Letters and Essays of Schiller;* trans. by J. Weiss, p. 202). Schiller continues: "On the other hand, Taste can avail true virtue, *positively*, in all the cases where the reason makes the first move, and is in danger of being outvoted by the stronger force of the native impulses. For, in this case, it reconciles our sensuousness with the interest of duty, and thus makes a meagre degree of moral volition adequate to the practice

The city which we seek is itself subject to a
standard. The catalogue of its virtues is the list
of its beauties; but its virtues and beauties are
both, to repeat Schiller's word, congruent with a
law. What is this law? The dimensions, we read,
of the city were such and such, "according to the
measure of a man, that is, of an angel"; the standard
to which we bring action and thought, morality and

of virtue. Now, if Taste, as such, injures true morality in no
case, but rather openly assists it in many, the circumstance that
it promotes in the highest degree, the *legality* of our conduct,
must possess great weight. Suppose that an æsthetic culture
could not in the least contribute to make us better intentioned,
it would, at any rate, render us skilful so to act, even without
a true moral intention, as a moral intention would have caused
us to act. It is true, our actions concern by no means the court
of morality, excepting as they are an expression of our intentions:
but, reversely, our intentions concern by no means the physical
court, and the plan of nature, excepting as they induce actions
which further the design of nature. But now both the physical
sphere of force, and the moral sphere of law, coincide so strictly,
and are so intimately blended, that actions which according to
their form coincide with a moral design, at the same time include
in their contents a coincidence with a physical design; and as the
whole natural structure only seems to exist in order to make goodness, the highest of all designs, possible, so goodness may in turn
be used as a means to sustain the natural structure. The order of
nature, then, is made dependent upon the morality of our intentions, and we cannot offend against the moral world without at
the same time producing disorder in the physical....An obligation
results...for us at least to satisfy the physical design by the
contents of our actions, even if we should not do as much for the
moral design by their *form*—at least to discharge to the design
of nature, as perfect instruments, the debt which we owe to
reason, as perfect Persons, in order not to be disgraced at the
same time before both tribunals."

art, is given by the proportions of that figure,
eternally pre-existent before all acts of mind or of
hand, the regulative norm by which they are judged,
the touchstone by which they are tried, but for ever
suffering the splendid abasement of successive in-
carnations in all acts congruent to his nature, acts
in which that nature is wrought by the art of
practised goodness, by the goodness of disciplined
art, to a vivid realisation in which system is vitalised
and life accepts self-governance in the control of
a unified Society.

CHAPTER IV

NOTES ON THE SIGNIFICANCE OF RHYTHM
IN PLATO'S SCHEME OF EDUCATION[1]

I propose to gather together some passages from Plato in which rhythm is discussed. To select them is a difficult task, for two reasons—first, that they are very numerous, and second, that to tear them from their setting is to rob them of part, at least, of their beauty, and, with their beauty, of their meaning. Many of the passages which I shall quote are, however, so familiar, that the context will easily be recalled, and for all I shall give references by which they may be restored to their proper places in the arguments in which they appear.

To begin with, there is the memorable passage in the *Laws*[2] (II, 653): "What men say is that the young of all creatures cannot be quiet in their bodies or in their voices; they are always wanting to move and cry out.... But whereas other animals have no perception of order or disorder in their movements, that is, of rhythm or harmony, as they are called, to us the Gods who, as we say, have been appointed to be our partners in the dance, have given the pleasurable sense of harmony and rhythm, and so

---

[1] Reprinted, with permission, from the *Journal of Experimental Pedagogy*.

[2] Jowett's translation in this and the following extracts.

they stir us with life, and we follow them and join hands with one another in dances and songs, and these they call choruses.... Shall we begin with the acknowledgment that education is first given through Apollo and the Muses?"

Here we note that the sense of harmony and rhythm is pleasurable; that it distinguishes men from other animals, that it is given to men by the Gods, that it prompts us to certain kinds of movement (dances, in which the Gods are our partners) and of utterance (viz., songs). And it would appear that the cultivation of this twofold sense is the business of education, itself a behest of Apollo and the Muses.

If we inquire more closely, as we must, what education is, we are at once told—it is "that training which is given by suitable habits to the first instincts of virtue in children, when pleasure and friendship and pain and hatred are rightly implanted in souls not yet capable of understanding the nature of them, and who find them, after they have attained reason, to be in harmony with her. This harmony of the soul, when perfected, is virtue; but the particular training in respect of pleasure and pain, which leads you always to hate what you ought to hate and love what you ought to love from the beginning to the end, may be separated off, and will be rightly called education."

There are, then, certain instincts of virtue in children; they are the rudiments of complete virtue, which is a harmony of the soul. Towards complete virtue we are led by a training which creates in us a habit of acting towards what is pleasant in one way, and in another towards what is painful, learning the while to entertain for what is pleasant the feeling of friendship, and towards what is painful that of hatred, and discovering at last that our habitual feelings and the actions which correspond with them are consonant with Reason. Education is a process of training in love and hatred, guided by authority, and ending in an ordered freedom for which the name is harmony.

Education is no process of technical equipment; it is a preparation for a life in which the fully-developed individual finds scope for his powers and realises himself in the society and in the service of his peers, his fellow-citizens. This is the work for which we must train our youth.

I quote next from the *Republic* III, 401: "If our youth are to do their work in life (they must) make...graces and harmonies their perpetual aim.... All life is full of them as well as every creative and constructive art, painting, weaving, embroidery, the art of building and the manufacture of vessels, as well as of the frames of animals and of plants—in all of them there is grace or the absence of grace. And absence of grace and inharmonious movement and discord are nearly allied to ill words and ill nature, as grace and harmony are the sisters of goodness and virtue and bear their likeness."

Grace and harmony are everywhere to be sought —not only in what we call the character and the conduct of men, but in all the works of their hands, in the arts and manufactures, and also in the structure and movement of animals and plants. They are the criteria of excellence, and are of kindred with goodness and virtue. It would not perhaps be amiss to speak of the virtue of a well-planned building or an exquisite tapestry, the goodness of a splendid horse or a lovely flower, since it is not amiss to speak of the beauty of right conduct or of noble character. Moral and aesthetic values are here brought very close together, if they are not indeed identified; and education is to be had in all the experiences which the world affords, for in all of them discrimination between good and bad, beautiful and ugly, pleasant and painful, must be made.

But some parts of education are specially valuable in themselves and specially useful as instruments of training since they are more completely under the control of the State itself, which is the chief agent in education, and of those of its ministry whose main duty is the care of the young. This part of education has two branches—Music and Gymnastic—conveniently separated one from the other, though Gymnastic is subordinate to Music, as the body exists for the sake of the soul. So we read (*Rep.* III, 401): "Musical training is a more potent instrument than any other, because rhythm and harmony find their way into the secret places of the soul, on which they mightily fasten, imparting grace, and making the soul graceful of him who is rightly educated, or ungraceful of him who is ill educated; and also because he who has received this true education of the inner being will most shrewdly perceive omissions or faults in art and nature."

The first instincts, as Plato calls them, of virtue, imply and depend for their existence and their development upon a certain critical quality, which discerns, through affections of pleasure and of pain, the good and the bad. It is to the fostering of these instincts that education directs itself; and the progress of education is measured by the gracefulness of the soul, which, becoming more and more graceful, becomes in the same process more and more critical.

The criterion of virtue and of beauty must be something personal and individual, a criterion based upon the pleasure or the pain of every person who can be moved by these affections. It is, it would seem, a question of taste, and about taste, whether in its simplest sense or in its most sublime meaning, there can be no argument. It is not easy for a man to describe a taste appreciated by his own palate; and if he did describe it in words satisfactory to himself and intelligible to another, it is not possible to prove that the taste which he describes as "sweet" or as "bitter," even though his neighbour acquiesces in the description, is the same taste which his neighbour detects and discriminates from others of his own palate. And yet for common agreement no appeal is more direct or convincing, and this not only in the physical realm, but in other realms open to human exploration. "Taste and see" we say about things to eat and drink—expecting agreement with our own taste, but not questioning the possibility, and, if it occurs, the propriety and genuineness of a taste different from our own. But these very words are used in an instance where genuine disagreement is not admitted as a thing to be conceived: "Taste and see that the LORD is good."

In this instance, it is imagined that difference is impossible; and the reply to a dissentient would be that he had not *really tasted* and seen. What it involves is not less than the claim that in the highest region judgment or taste is at once intimately personal and at the same time common and, indeed, universal—unless we say that some tastes are denied to some capacities, or, with less risk of provoking opposition, that some capacities are less large and less sensitive than others in certain respects. And if we accept either of these alternatives, we should find it convenient to give to those persons in whom the apprehension, capacity or taste in question exists, or exists in a high degree of discrimination, some special name. We cannot call them religious persons, without confusion; we may perhaps, at any rate for the moment, call them saints.

To the considerations just raised we may presently return. The critical mind criticizes even the instrument which is intended to increase his critical power. Music is such an instrument—music including letters, poetry, history, rhetoric and every kind of art—but music itself is judged; and we have to ask by what standard it is to be judged. Clearly there can be but one, namely, pleasure. I quote again (*Laws* v, 658): "The excellence of music is to be measured by pleasure. But the pleasure must not be that of chance persons; the fairest music is that which delights the best and best educated, and especially that which delights the one man who is pre-eminent in virtue and education."

This is surely argument in a circle. Perhaps it is; but perhaps it is argument, so to speak, in a spiral: we have come round, not, in fact, to our starting point, but to a point vertically above it. We have now a fresh inquiry: "where is the man pre-eminent in virtue and education?" and yet another: "how are we to recognize him?"

We may be aided in our search for him, if we can in imaginative forecast present him to our minds. The quality and the preparation of the truly musical person are set before us in such a passage as that in *Rep.* III, 402: "Neither we nor our guardians whom we have to educate can ever become musical until we and they know the essential forms of temperance, courage, liberality, magnificence, and their kindred, as well as the contrary forms, in all their combinations, and can recognise them and their images wherever they are found, not slighting them in small things or great, but believing them all to be within the sphere of one art and study." It is clear that the educated man draws into a single art or study all the lesser arts as we know them by their several names, and also the elements of what we call morality or virtue; and everywhere "in small things or great" he will be quick to perceive the presence or the image of artistic or of moral law. And this habit of mind by which he harmonises goodness and beauty may have, indeed must have, a similar effect of harmony upon himself, compact as he is of body and soul. So Plato continues: "And when a beautiful soul harmonizes with a beautiful form, and the two are cast in one mould, that will be the fairest of sights to him who has an eye to contemplate the vision. And the fairest is also the loveliest, and the man who has the spirit of harmony will be most in love with the loveliest."

To him who has an "eye to contemplate" the vision will be granted.

Who, we may ask, is to enjoy the spectacle, to gaze upon "the fairest of sights"? It is only he who is himself of kindred with that upon which he looks, whose own soul, fitly mated with a beautiful form, has been moulded to the fashion of the spiritual beauty which he contemplates. Such a seer will blend the temper of admiration or even of adoration with that of criticism or even of scepticism. He will not yield, he will feel indeed no temptation to yield to a flaccid sentiment of vague and valueless admiration; he will not offer exuberant praise where modest commendation is appropriate, nor polite acquiescence where repugnance and condemnation should be provoked. He will exhibit, because he will possess, the character of the watchdog. Philosophic, he will distinguish his friends from his foes;

but he will very happily admit that his foes are
strangers, and quickly discover that to bring them
into friendship all that is needed is that he should
come to know them.   He will love knowledge, and
not less the process of getting knowledge, and the
transformation which he achieves in turning the
unknown and the hostile into the well-known ally
and friend will delight him, not only by its result,
but as it proceeds.   For his scepticism is not a
negative thing: it is creative.   Looking shrewdly
at or through the form of the stranger, he penetrates
to his heart, and there finds, what he postulates,
something to recognise—something which he had
known before, but which was for a moment hidden
from him.   The knowledge of good and of evil,
fearlessly pursued by ingenuous minds, turns out to
be knowledge of good, residing unimpaired at the
heart of things, and revealing itself at last to friendly
eyes, and with a triumphant self-surrender trans-
fusing the veils which obscured it, reshaping the
misshapen form that held it, to accept and return
the welcome of the philosophic mind.

How, then, is this character, this mind, to be
brought into being, and by what training is it to be
brought to its just perfection?   This is the business
of education, a national concern, entrusted to the
guardians of society.   It is to be observed that the
guardians have something to safeguard: a society,
a state, has been established, and such stability as
it has it owes to its conformity to certain laws.   Its
stability is threatened by the invasion of lawlessness,

which may either take the state by storm, or—a
subtler and more serious peril—creep in upon it
stealthily and by almost imperceptible degrees.
Against the danger the guardians (*Rep.* IV, 425)
must build a fortress, and lay its foundations in
music. The beginning of music will, for children,
include their games, their stories, told to them or
made up by themselves, and all the show that they
put into their little stage of make-believe. They
must learn to play prettily, and simply; their play
must be of a law-abiding kind; so that thus early,
and before they have been able to see the reason for
it, they may have got the habit of orderliness. They
may then rediscover, what Plato complains had been
lost in his day, the "minor moralities," as Dr Bosan-
quet brilliantly renders his words. "What are
these?" the question is asked; and the answer is
worth quotation: "The proper habits of silence in
the young before their elders, and offering them a
seat, and standing up when they enter, and respect
for parents, and haircutting, and dress and shoes,
and, in general, the personal appearance and everything of that kind." All this is not matter for
legislation; it is to be secured through the discipline
of common sense used lightly with imaginative
freedom, used firmly with religious severity by
parents or teachers, who, respecting themselves,
respect their children also, and pay in advance a
tribute to the understanding which they will one
day possess, by making them obey a law which they
do not yet comprehend. So education is begun, by

the imposition of law at the hands of authority, an imposition so relentless that not even the spontaneous play of children escapes its control, yet so gentle and wise that play is not robbed of its natural gaiety. The reason of the law, it is perhaps not unnecessary to repeat, is not within the understanding of those on whom it is imposed.

Plato never adopted the consecutive arrangement of topics illustrated by the writers of text-books for examinations, and here, following his own inspiration, he turns at once from the beginning to the end of education. What more have we to do—he himself raises the question, reverting now to themes with which he has been occupied before he wrote down the passage to which I have just now made reference—what more have we to do in our legislation? We have to accept for ourselves with the easy and cheerful dutifulness of disciplined children the enactments of an authority which we understand as little as they understand that which constrains them. "Nothing remains for us; but for Apollo, the God of Delphi, there remains the ordering of the greatest and noblest and chiefest things of all...." "The institutions of temples and sacrifices, and the entire service of gods, demigods, and heroes; also the ordering of the repositories of the dead, and the rites which have to be observed by him who would propitiate the inhabitants of the world below. These are matters of which we are ignorant ourselves, and as founders of a city we should be unwise in trusting them to any interpreter but our ancestral deity. He is the god who sits in the centre, on the navel of the earth, and he is the interpreter of religion to all mankind " (*Rep.* IV, 429).

I shall not now inquire whether or not this is paradox, this ending of a process by which the mind is trained to the use of reason in the unquestioning acceptance of a ritual, consecrated by tradition, enriched by unbroken observance, as the fixed form of reverence paid to things of which, as Plato puts it, "we are ignorant." It is, I think, at any rate clear that for Plato this was no paradox. He is guiltless of the mean logic which calls itself consistency, and is consistent only in its constant insensibility to the throbbing, vitalizing darkness which surrounds the lucid realm of reason and by closing gives it definition.

We find from reflection on the passages which have now been cited that a space is marked out in which freedom, guided by intelligence, has its sphere; and that this space is bounded on either side, at the beginning and at the end, by authority which is to be obeyed. This authority is to be obeyed in ignorance, but we have to remark that this is an ignorance which does not violate freedom or damage intelligence. For children acquire and learn to use the gifts and arts of freedom under the direction of a control which, at first external to themselves, they gradually make their own as they become truly members of the society into which they are born; and this control, by curbing licence, indicates the avenues in which power may be well employed, and by offering the contrast between fruitful and fruitless effort makes the nascent intelligence aware of itself. And when such freedom as men may enjoy, used with intelligence, quickened and matured by experience, has reached what seems to younger eyes a range unlimited, there is revealed to eyes refreshed by wisdom and undimmed by experience a limit set by law, to be admitted and revered, not as a hard boundary against which the baffled will may break itself in impetuous and impotent assault, but as the condition upon which ordered activity depends. This measured sway from control to control, through a broadening tract of freedom, is rhythm conceived in its largest terms. This, if I understand aright some passages which will presently be quoted (and many others which seem to bear the same sense might very easily be added), is what Plato calls *good* rhythm. It alone justly deserves the name, but to distinguish it, where distinction is very need- ful, from counterfeits, he gives this the name of *good*. The counterfeits he calls *bad rhythms*. We have therefore to inquire what is the difference between good and bad rhythms. In both we are to recognise the action and reaction of freedom and of control; but in the good, control and freedom are kindred from the first, and time and experience discover more and more fully the intimacy of their relation; whereas in the bad, control is mere necessity and freedom mere licentiousness.

Let us take first a passage from *Rep.* III, 400: "Grace, or the absence of grace, is the effect of good **or** bad rhythm accompanying good or bad style,

and the same is true of good or bad harmony; for
our principle is that rhythm and harmony are regu-
lated by the words and not the words by them....
The words and the character of the style will depend
on the temper of the soul, and everything else on the
style.   Good language and harmony and grace and
rhythm depend on simplicity.   I mean the simplicity
of a truly and nobly ordered mind, not that other
simplicity which is only a euphemism for folly."
If for *words* we say *meaning*, the interpretation of
the passage is made clear.   Significance must determine form, and form must obey and express significance.   This is not to say that we can translate into
words the meaning of a piece of music, or render a
poem into prose; but it is to say that some meaning
must be there, and that the form is, if it is perfect,
the one apt expression for that meaning.   Again, it
is the meaning of a mind which by a noble discipline
has attained simplicity.

    The same doctrine appears to be maintained in
a well-known passage of the *Laws* (ii, 656–7), where
Plato describes the regulations enforced in Egypt in
regard to music and dancing.   "I know," he says,
"other things in Egypt are not so good; but what
I tell you about music is true and deserving of consideration....What are the laws about music and
dancing in Egypt?   You will wonder when I tell
you.   Long ago they appear to have recognised the
very principle of which we are now speaking—that
their young citizens must be habituated to forms and
strains of virtue.   These they fixed, and exhibited

the patterns of them in their temples; and no
painter or artist is allowed to innovate upon them,
or to leave the traditional forms and invent new
ones...no alteration is allowed in these arts, or in
music at all." Let us interrupt Plato for a moment.
Clearly he maintains that modes of dancing and of
music are the expression of character, but not the
expression merely of individual character; they are
that, but they are more than that. They are the
expression of a national character, which the individual takes on himself as he comes to complete
self-understanding and self-development—an expression, settled by use, sanctioned by authority,
and yet consistent with the individuality of those
who in successive ages adopt it, an expression which
indeed serves the double purpose of maintaining
unimpaired the character of the society in which
and for the uses of which it has been formulated,
and within the general framework of that social or
national character, of providing the opportunity to
its members of realizing their oneness with society
while carrying to the utmost limits of ordered
originality their personal qualities. There may be
varieties of style within the common convention.
The sentences which follow demand and deserve
a close study: "A lawgiver," Plato continues,
"may institute Melodies which have a natural truth
and correctness without any fear of failure." This
surely is a great claim to make for the lawgiver.
Let us note that he is a lawgiver, handing on to
others what he has himself received. "To do this"

—I resume the quotation—"must be the work of GOD, or a divine person." The careful reader will not miss the reverent irony, the humorous submission, the effrontery of faith, in the concluding lines: "In Egypt they have a tradition that their ancient chants are the composition of the goddess Isis. And...if a person can only find in any way the natural melodies, he may confidently embody them in a fixed and legal form."

To guard ourselves against the risk of misunderstanding Plato when he speaks about the lawgiver, we must remember that for the Greek States the name of a half-legendary, half-historical, and remote founder was associated with the ideas which for us are called to mind by the word constitution. To violate the constitution, if we may pass from the language of our own time to the figurative language held by Plato, is to disobey the lawgiver.

It is hardly a contemporary person of whom he speaks, but rather of a person to whom distance has lent a certain enchantment and dignity. Yet the functions of the traditional lawgiver are to be fulfilled by officers of the State, of whom the most important (*Laws* VI, 765–6) is the Minister of Education, who is concerned not with a department of national or of social life, but with the whole of it, and is the representative to his contemporaries of the traditional lawgiver, and dependent like him for the successful discharge of his duties on nothing less than the inspiration of the gods.

In a memorable passage of the *Republic* (III, 395)

Plato[1] tells us that the Guardians of the State are to be "consummate artificers of freedom," and it is because they are the living depositaries of tradition that they achieve for the State the liberty which it must have if its obedience to law is to be vital. Here again we have the same great principles of rhythm illustrated. The resultant of control and of self-expression is not the resultant of opposed but of combined forces.

To this consideration we may presently return. At present we remark that education is a sacred and serious occupation, because it is an artistic occupation. Before choosing your minister of education you resort to the temple of Apollo. The doctrine put forward in some of the passages already cited, that the rules or laws of art are a kind of nature, or a principle of life, suggests or is suggested by another doctrine of wider scope. It is that life itself is an art. In an early passage of the *Republic* (I, 342 *et seq.*), Plato speaks about the disinterestedness of art, and here he is thinking of the several professions and occupations of men—the art of the shepherd, or the art of the practitioner in any department of human activity. There is a general art of life in which all men are engaged both as individuals and also as members of a community which embraces them. The lawgiver is he who sets the music, who gives the tone and determines the modes of this supreme art. He is the subject of a sacred frenzy in which order, become habitual, is

[1] See also IV, 421.

raised to the level of passion, and he is entitled to impose his command upon lesser men than himself because he is himself clothed with an authority not his own. It was apparently a circumstance not unknown in Greece, that small offices should seem to give immense importance to still smaller men, who, to adopt Plato's image, believed themselves to be six feet high, because flatterers, built upon an even lower scale, continually told them that they were of that very respectable height. But the true lawgiver is like the poet; indeed he moves upon a larger and a loftier plane: with the gods or the heroes we may dare to compare him. The poet, says Plato (*Ion*, p. 534), "brings songs from honeyed fountains, culling them out of the gardens and dells of the muses; like a bee, he wings his way from flower to flower. The poet is a light and winged and holy thing, and there is no invention in him until he is inspired and is out of his senses and the mind is no longer in him; when he has not attained to this state he is powerless and unable to utter his oracles." A further passage from the same dialogue emphasizes the same teaching, and supplies an example. "GOD takes away the minds of poets and uses them as his ministers, as he also uses diviners and holy prophets in order that we who hear them may know them to be speaking not of themselves who utter these priceless words in a state of unconsciousness, but that GOD himself is the speaker, and that through them he is conversing with us. And Tynnichus, the Chalcidian, affords us a striking instance of what I am saying: he wrote nothing that anyone would care to remember but the famous paean which is in everyone's mouth, one of the finest poems ever written, simply an invention of the Muses, as he himself says." The lawgiver is numbered among these diviners and holy prophets.

In the ordered state, the embodied harmony of human activities, there will be differences of function, and the differences will be recognised. On this Plato insists, as everyone remembers, with much gravity in the *Republic*. The stability of the state, he tells us, can only be maintained if everyone will mind his own business, and confine himself to that. And every man being governed by the conditions of his occupation will express himself in accordance with it. It is true that above the particular occupation or calling in which he is engaged, he has to practise the general art of life; but for the most part, he will avoid mistakes in life if he fulfils the claims and performs the duties of that station in which he is placed. But if the citizens are eager to remind themselves that they are human beings first and practitioners of the several arts after that, let them at least note that even if they are human beings, they must be either male or female, and not traverse the natural boundaries of their sex. In the *Laws* (VII, 802–3), an illustration not common in this context is used. "We must distinguish," we read, "and determine on some general principle what songs are suitable to women and what to men, and must assign to them the proper melodies and

rhythms.   It is shocking for a whole harmony (the
harmony of society as a whole is meant) to be in-
harmonical, or for a rhythm to be unrhythmical....
Now both sexes have melodies and rhythm which
of necessity belong to them, and those of women are
clearly enough indicated by their natural difference."
In an earlier passage of the same dialogue (*Laws* II,
669) Plato contends that the Muses themselves would
never make the mistake of confounding what is
appropriate for men with what is suitable to women;
but poets, being very much inferior to the Muses in
character, make this, as he regards it, monstrous
blunder.

Rhythm (*Laws* V, 665), Plato tells us, is the order
of motion.   It is motion given by freedom, but
exercised under control.   There need be no opposition between freedom and control, and when
rhythm is good there is none.   When rhythm is
bad, control, as we have seen, is a gentle name for
mere coercion.   But if there is no essential opposition,
there is still contrast between freedom and control.
Motion implies a goal, not yet reached; control
suggests the negation of motion.   It is what Plato
calls rest, or inactivity.   Let me quote a difficult
passage from Theaetetus in illustration (*Theaet.* 153).
We may easily see that "motion is the source of that
which is said to be and become, and rest of not-
being and destruction; for fire and warmth, which
are supposed to be the parent and nurse of all other
things, are born of friction, which is a kind of motion
...and this is the origin of fire.   And the race of

animals is generated in the same way. And is not bodily habit spoiled by rest and idleness, but preserved for a long time by motion and exercise? And so...of the mental habit. Is not the soul informed and improved and preserved by thought and attention, which are motions; but when at rest, unstirred by thought or attention, the soul is uninformed and speedily forgets whatever she has learned."

Control means direction, it may be urged; but direction implies choice, and choice means rejection as well as acceptance. Command is at the same time an order to do this and an order not to do that. It is this contrast that Plato illustrates; but not this alone. Motion, as we have seen, implies desire; but what when desire is fulfilled? Will motion be possible, is it conceivable then? Progress implies a destination; what when the destination is reached? Our notion of goodness seems to include the notion of progress. Will goodness cease to be itself when it has reached perfection? And again, rest means cessation from activity; yet rest is sought. We think of the alternation of rest and activity; it is one of the forms of the rhythmic balance of freedom and control, but may we not speak of the goal of endeavour as a repose which will never be disturbed; and if so, have we set before ourselves a mere negation as our end?

The question is asked, the dilemma stated, with indignant eloquence in the *Sophistes* (249): "O heavens, can we ever be made to believe that motion and life and soul are not present with absolute Being?

Can we imagine Being (the fulfilment, that is, a perfection of all the objects of our effort and hope) to
be devoid of life and mind, and to remain in awful
unmeaningness, an everlasting fixture?... Or shall
we say that Being has mind and not life... Or both,
but that there is no soul in which they exist.... Or
that Being has mind and life and soul, but that
although endowed with soul remains entirely un-
moved?... Then our inference is that, if there is no
motion, neither is there any mind anywhere or about
anything or belonging to anyone.... And yet this
equally follows, if we grant that all things are in
motion, upon this view too, mind has no existence."

The answer to the problem is suggested later in
the same dialogue (*Sophistes* 250): "Then you can
conceive of Being as some third and distinct nature,
under which rest and motion are included, and
observing that they both participate in Being, you
declare that they are.... Being surely has communion
with both of them."

So motion ends in passionate repose; and rest
becomes instinct with tranquil emotion: the happy
rivalry of contrasted forces is composed in a life
which has the simplicity of art, and seeks nothing
but the undisturbed communion of the mind with
itself.

CHAPTER V

ORATORY AND VIRTUE

When Quintilian boldly asserts that the perfect orator must be a good man, he claims that his Treatise on the Art of Oratory is a Treatise on Education. The orator, he says, must not only have consummate ability in speaking, but every excellence of mind, and it is clear that in excellence he includes virtue. There are those, he adds, who would leave ethics to philosophers, and many writers on oratory have supported this view, believing that it was their business to add eloquence as a final and crowning accomplishment to persons who had received from other teachers other and distinct kinds of learning. The study of speech had come indeed long before his time to be divorced from the study of things about which men speak. The tongue became an instrument of gain, and men who were esteemed eloquent abandoned the care of morals which were thus neglected to become the prize of the less robust intellects. He carries his accurate irony still further when he adds that some persons, disliking the labour of cultivating eloquence, turn

back as upon an easier task upon the discipline of
the mind, and the establishment of rules of life. For
his own part he is unwilling to make a severance
between things which are naturally allied. He does
not say that every good man must be an orator,
but he comes very near to making that startling
announcement, for the orator is described as a man
who has to sustain his character as a citizen: he
must be qualified for the management of public
affairs, able to govern communities by his counsel,
settle them by means of laws, and improve them by
judicial enactments. Already when Quintilian wrote,
the duties and powers of a citizen were limited to
a much narrower range; he has set forth what had
been and what he would still desire, not what actually
was in Rome and the Roman world as he knew it;
the word citizen had fallen both from its ancient
glory and from its proper significance. Yet he is
fain to argue that the orator is for him the citizen
at his height, at his fullest development: he is the
ideal citizen, and might well claim kindred with him
whom a liberal education as Milton conceived it
made able justly and magnanimously to fulfil all
offices both of peace and of war.

The education of the young has at all times been
the touchstone of civilization: it is the attempt of
Age to justify its ways to Youth; it is the apology
of the present to the future—its splendid vindication
or its timid and paltering excuse. No doubt, this
effort at self-explanation has often been half-con-
scious and quite unsystematic, though at some

brilliant epochs what had been dimly felt by a whole
people was brought by a speaker or writer to luminous
expression and so received a force and a direction
which it would else have lacked. This consummate
expression has again and again been like the bloom-
ing of a rare flower which attains perfection and is
overtaken by decay at the same instant; but always,
whether splendidly revealed or faintly suggested, we
have in any sincere utterance of a national ideal the
best record that a community can leave us of its aim
in education, and in its scheme of education the
most trustworthy account of its corporate and collective ambition.

Such an ideal can never be wholly frustrated;
and indeed, when it has prompted and been quickened by words in which at once its meaning is made
public and its secret enshrined, it may be said, in
a sense, to have reached completion. A national
pride tempered by comity; a personal dignity maintained with sweetness; a versatility which consorts
with real strength of character; the daring which
springs from buoyant and disciplined health; fit-
ness for the labours of warfare, and the intelligence
to enjoy, without softness, a cultured peace—a vivid
appreciation of beauty, as an active principle ordering
and informing private and public conduct; and as
a crown, modesty—the sense of proportion—humour
blent with reverence—all this, or something like this,
was what the Athenians at the period of their
supreme success desired to possess, and hoped they
had. And the orator who interpreted this ambition

framed for them, and not for them alone, a code for
the education of the young.

The Romans, with a wider horizon, though with
a vision less acute, translated this language of the
Greeks into their own tongue to suit the needs of an
Empire which the Greeks had dreamt of, but never
realised. And once more we find an ideal drawn of
the citizen, prepared for war and for peace, the
inheritor now of Hellenic culture, occupied in government but making leisure for speculation, and uniting
the qualities of the statesman with those of the
scholar.

The picture is drawn by the orator, but he is its
original; and in rendering to the State an interpretation which it accepted of its own traditions and
hopes, he stands out as the model and the teacher
of youth.

It has been maintained by some distinguished
writers on style, themselves practised orators, that
a main difficulty of beginners is to be found merely
in lack of matter. If they had anything to say—
that is the blunt contention—they would soon find
how to say it. To know what to say is, no doubt,
a large part of the equipment of the orator. Cicero
himself was arrested for a moment by this truism.
It was of course a tempting doctrine to a speaker
and writer whose range was from the Nature of
the Gods to the pettiest business of the law courts.
He had spoken with effect upon every imaginable
subject: he must, then, possess a knowledge as
encyclopaedic as his topics had been various. But

though he was never unwilling to set high store by
his natural endowments, he was bound to remember
that his mind had been enriched by scholarship, and
his speech, facile always, rendered apt and cogent by
training. He was ready, therefore, to admit that,
while he owed much to nature, he owed much also
to the discipline of long years which had taught him
the full use of his powers; and he agreed that for
the orator learning was necessary, as well as training
in the art of speech.

"No one," we learn, "can be a real orator in the
full sense of the word unless he first acquires a knowledge of all the great subjects of human study."
And that this knowledge was to be nothing super-
ficial we discover when we are told that "the true
virtue of rhetoric cannot have full play unless the
speaker has mastered the subject on which he intends
to speak." And with knowledge so manifold and
profound the orator is "to express himself in a style
at once impressive and artistic and conformable with
the thoughts and feelings of human nature." It is
true, the subjects of knowledge were then both fewer
and less exploited than in our own time; but even
so, the task would seem to demand more than ordinary gifts, and Cicero confesses as much himself.
"It is," he says, "a labour of incalculable and infinite
difficulty." The standard of unlimited knowledge
and of eloquence appropriate to it was felt to be an
ideal, not to be attained, but yet useful for directing
ambition, for guiding practice, and perhaps for
fostering modesty. This, at least, seems to be

suggested by a fine sentence in which we read that there are some subjects of which even an accomplished orator "may enjoy the privilege of ignorance."

The orator, indeed, may be described as the educated man who must live by his skill and learning, but must appeal not only to his peers but to others who are more directly concerned in affairs. He is, in effect, an interpreter between these two groups, understanding the interests of both, and speaking a tongue satisfactory to one and intelligible to the other. He represents in a high and perhaps a unique degree the culture of his nation; he is neither the pedant nor the mere man of business. He comes near to combining the qualities ascribed by Earle to the "downright scholar" with those of the "contemplative man." "The hermitage of his study" may have "made him," when he sets out in the world, "somewhat uncouth" in the eyes of men whose manners are a bright but thin veneer, "but practise him a little in men and brush him over with good company, and he shall outbalance those glisterers as far as a solid substance does a feather or gold gold lace." "He is a scholar in this great University of the World, and the same his book and study. He cloisters not his meditations in the narrow darkness of a room, but sends them abroad with his eyes, and his brain travels with his feet."

The orator, active and influential in the affairs of the moment, apprehending their import more completely than others because, though engaged, he was not to be absorbed in them; approaching them with the enthusiasm of a politician, but considering them with the serenity of a student—the orator was for the Greeks and the Romans the living canon and standard of national education. He was to discover to his fellow-citizens their true aspirations, and by fitly expressing them to give them definition and clearness in the public mind, and so to hasten their fulfilment.

In later times, as well as in those which I have tried to recall, great speakers have held a similar position. But these instances are enough for the present purpose. They serve to show that the orator was a public teacher, that it was his business to appreciate and to embody the national or civic sentiment. And in such communities as we have been thinking of, small and compact as they are, communities in which it was possible for all citizens to take a direct and active part in government, it was, of course, the ambition of every youth to become a capable speaker. Below the orator, and preparing for the work which he was to do in the education of the young citizen, there were, naturally, teachers of subordinate rank; but their work was controlled and directed by his. We have, therefore, a system of education in which oratory was regarded not simply as the gift of the few, but as a necessary qualification for all who were to take a proper part in a citizen's life.

And we must note that for the making of the orator there were three requisites, named in order

of logical importance, natural ability, learning, and
training in speech. Natural ability must clearly
have meant a quick sensitiveness to the temper of
the time, a readiness to understand both books
and men, a certain vigour and alertness of mind.
Its value needs no argument, but it is remarkable
that in societies where eloquent and powerful speech
was so highly rated, and its results so important,
the necessity for learning, for knowledge of many
kinds laboriously acquired, should have been so
clearly perceived, and that even speech itself, however fluent and copious, was felt to be inadequate
and ineffective unless it were disciplined and matured
by study.

The orator must, besides natural parts, have
knowledge and that retirement of mind which is
the first fruit of study; he must have readiness to
understand the language of those whose interests
are not like his own, and to find kinship in difference;
he must learn, without spoiling it, to adapt his
speech to their intelligence; he must be an advocate
of the ideals of his time and country, but with
reserves and with sincerity; he must be a man of
books, but the world must be his University.

To speak well is to have enjoyed experience of
the subject treated in speech, and then to review and
order experience, lifting it thus into a higher plane
of reality than mere experience unreviewed and un-
ordered by the mind could possess. But this revival
and rearrangement of experience, wrought by the
reflective mind, is also action the most intense and

vivid. In a special form we conventionally call it drama, and drama, as Aristotle simply put it, is doing things. But it is doing things over again upon the stage of the mind, and setting them there beyond the dominion of time and place and accident, giving them there an eternal because an artistic quality.

This rendering of experience, this recall of emotion for its very spiritual intensity, must govern and limit itself by strict rules of art which give form to what was amorphous, and definition and clearness to what was once vague and inexact, rules consonant with the process itself, and necessary to it because of its essence. Speech, then, is thought shaped and lined by art; it is life relived with the precision which conscious enjoyment allows; it is the speaker himself surveyed by his own criticism, and now made more intimately himself by the detachment granted to self-knowledge.

But art tempts artifice, and counterfeit closely attends the genuine product of the soul. The detachment of which we have just spoken is one with self-realisation; it is granted to a man who looks not into a mirror, with eyes of complacency or of disappointment, but into his heart with an imagination dauntless and in its serenity impassioned. Yet courage implies control, and serenity is won by discipline; what wonder, then, if the semblance of courage is achieved by mechanical devices, and the appearance of serenity by faces which have put on convention like a mask!

Psychologists tell us that if we would become possessed of certain emotions we should act as if we already possessed them; we should do kind acts and wear a benevolent aspect if we wish to be kind and benevolent at heart. If this is a true, it is also a dangerous doctrine. For we may grow so adept in conduct, we may fix our faces so rigidly in a smile, as to find it easier to repeat the applauded deed and retain the welcomed expression, than to stir into being the generous sentiments of which they should become the symbols as well as the precursors and heralds.

It is here that we find the common distinction justified between manners and morals; manners the well-known formulae on which the world insists, morals the hidden motives of the heart. And it is not difficult to think of a youth or a maiden learning, under the direction of a well-paid tutor or governess, the manners of polite society, and yet missing a polish like that of a precious stone, which by attrition is made to reveal the glowing colour at its heart, its inwrought grain and delicacy of exquisite texture.

So speech and practice of speech came to be dissociated from thought and life: and hence the contumely heaped upon those who with little capacity for vehement thought or for reflective life, devoted their dull gifts, equally fleshless and un-spiritualised, to the cultivation of what they called style. "I have"—so Locke[1] declares—"seldom or never observed any one to get the skill of Reasoning

[1] Locke, *Thoughts* (Camb. Press, 1902), p. 162, etc., §§ 188, 189.

well, or speaking handsomely, by studying those rules which pretend to teach it.... Right Reasoning is founded on something else than the *Predicaments* and *Predicables*, and does not consist in talking in *Mode* and *Figure* itself." Yet he is bound to add, "If you would have your Son *reason well*, let him read *Chillingworth*; and if you would have him speak well, let him be conversant in *Tully*, to give him the true *Idea of Eloquence*; and let him read those things which are well writ in *English*, to perfect his style in the Purity of our Language." And keeping in mind the writers he has named, and others comparable with them, he explains at once what is the true Idea of Eloquence. "If the Use and End of right Reasoning be to have right Notions and a right Judgment of Things, to distinguish between Truth and Falsehood, Right and Wrong, and to act accordingly, be sure not to let your Son be bred up in the Art and Formality of disputing, either practising it himself, or admiring it in others.... Truth is to be found and supported by a mature and due Consideration of Things themselves, and not by artificial Terms and Ways of arguing."

Clearly then the reading of Chillingworth is held likely to assist good reasoning, and the study of Cicero will help a student not merely to speak well, but to get the true idea of Eloquence, a pre-requisite for excellent speech; and once more, though artificial Terms and Ways of Arguing are held up for derision, it is granted that for the discovery of Truth, for the acquiring of right notions and a right judgment of

Things, what is needed is a mature and due consideration of Things themselves. But these "Things
themselves" are encountered in the region of thought,
where the mind discoursing with itself holds precise
argument with other minds, and bends to its own
peculiar and individual uses the symbols which
custom has invested with common significance.

Even in the humbler modes of speech we desire
to be understood by our hearers and by ourselves,
and Locke admits that "to write and speak correctly
gives a grace and gains a favourable attention to
what one has to say."

Other forms of oratory are distinguished from
that in which its aim is persuasion; narrative,
analysis, explanation may in turn occupy the orator;
and yet we may properly claim that his constant
business and pre-occupation is to persuade, to carry
his hearers with him through record and examination, through inquiry and proof, to some conclusion
which he regards as Truth and calls by that name,
and to convince those who have been willing or com-
pelled companions in his journey that he is indeed
at last arrived at his goal, and that the goal is what
he has named it. And whatever his special subject
may be, it is of value to him and to them only in as
much as it is, I will not say related to, but identified
with the common and ordinary concerns of men who,
entertaining the forceful emotions of love or hate,
are driven by thought upon action.

Elyot, paraphrasing a passage to which our
attention has already been drawn, strongly urges

this lesson. "Tulli," he says in the Book called the *Governour*[1], "Tulli affirmed that a man may not be an oratour heaped with praise but if he have gotten the knowledge of all things and arts of greatest importance. And how shall an oratour speak of that thynge that he hath not learned?" The knowledge of all things is hard to come by; and perhaps we have stumbled, as Plato pleasantly puts it, upon the reason why orators are scarce. But the fact is that it is the plural that imagination boggles at. The truth which Cicero and Elyot after him attempt to set forth is more concisely, but not less lucidly, given in a sentence of Jowett: "A common cause[2] of failure is ignorance of the world." If then for "knowledge of all things" we substitute "knowledge of the world" we shall be intelligible; for here we have a whole which is other and greater than its parts, and may be embraced by persons whose experience of things may be limited to a narrow range of instances, but who have won their way to reason and right notions, by a due and mature consideration of such things as they have known.

I have not yet attempted a definition of oratory, but rather have tried to look at it from some points of view suggested in part at least by several writers whom I have named. To all of them it seems to mean something more than deft handling of words; indeed they contrast it with that, whether they regard formal exercises in language as preparatory

[1] Elyot, *Governour*, I, xiii
[2] Jowett, *College Sermons* (Murray, 1896), p. 259.

to it or as likely to mislead those who seek it. With all of them, it means or comes near to meaning an efficient and practical wisdom, forged of experience and tempered to expression, like some very fine instrument fitting perfectly to a hand, which in its deft mastery moves like thought incarnate, an instrument too which so shrewdly deals with its material that by marking it seems to create it, and to be the cause of the apt and intricate articulation which it indicates. It is, truly, composition, the putting of things together, but composition upon a heroic, or as one may dare to say, a divine scale. For ordinarily we think of composition as implying arrangement, of course; but arrangement after selection made of materials appropriate for some purpose; and such selection involves the rejection of whatever is confessed inappropriate to the business in hand. But "nothing"—we may recall once more at this stage Quintilian's pregnant aphorism— "nothing is unnecessary to the orator." His canvas is as wide as the satirist's, "quidquid agunt homines"; though his treatment, as we shall see, is different. Two passages from Sadoleto's *de Pueris recte Instituendis* may here be quoted in illustration.

"Now the very starting point of our course is the art of Grammar; when you have devoted yourself to it as much as is needful, you must leave it in order to adorn and cultivate your style by the aid of another art or discipline of the first importance and the greatest distinction, the pursuit of which claims all the remainder of our lives, for without it

no man can well attain greatness or eminence among
his fellows either at home in peace or abroad in war.
This training in dignified, clear and polished speech
upon any subject which may be proposed should, in
my view, accompany a youth throughout every stage
of his development so that it may be carried along
with him as he advances towards philosophy, as a
river is borne towards the sea, and at last becomes
merged and identified with the element into which
it passes. At the same time I would have his
rhetoric flow onward in a stream ever enriched by
the tributary gifts of the other arts and disciplines."

Here, as it seems to me, Sadoleto perhaps deliberately mixes his metaphors, or should we perhaps
say, he passes on from one metaphor to another
inconsistent with the first. In the first oratory, and
training in oratory, is a river flowing on to a sea,
philosophy or wisdom, in which by losing itself it
finds fulfilment and perfection; in the second,
rhetoric is likened to a great stream receiving in its
course the tribute of confluent waters, the other
arts and sciences, which surely are the elements of
wisdom itself.

But let us turn to the other passage which almost
immediately follows:

"The ancient Greeks dealt with this question more
elaborately and at greater leisure than our own
countrymen; they perceived that the road to that
complete and supreme wisdom which they believed
exhibited itself in statesmanship and pre-eminence
of judgment and eloquence lay through arts of this

kind. They appointed men as teachers at once of
oratory and of philosophy, whom they called
Sophists, masters, as we may say, of Civic wisdom,
and engaged their services at a recognised fee for
their children."

Complete wisdom, perfectly presented in its
proper forms, is made one with the forms of its
inevitable and natural choice, and these forms are
themselves made one, since each of them, equally
with the others, is the body, touched and fired by
a spiritual sensitivity, of wisdom now made manifest.
What are these coequal forms? They are statesmanship, pre-eminence in judgment, and eloquence or
oratory. The teacher of oratory is the teacher of
Civic Wisdom, or knowledge of the world.

We have no difficulty now in discerning the
difference between the method of the satirist and
that of the orator. "All the doings of men," in all
their baffling and inconceivable contrariety, "make
up the medley," the hotch-potch, of the satirist's
book. He rejects nothing, but he essays no re-
conciliations—arrogance and humility, wealth that
intoxicates or cloys, poverty that hardens or deforms,
affection or dislike, impulses of generosity and sordid
meanness, the proud joy of life, the quelling humilia-
tion of death, honour and infamy heaped on honour
to extinguish it by the murderous hands of kinsmen
turned to foes, shame disclosing at its heart something
of tenderness or even of nobility—all these are
figures in the crowd that makes its way through
his pages, and he himself who has bared them of

every robe or rag of pretension or concealment,
stands aside, more remote than a judge who in con-
demning appeals to a common standard known even
when denied, and in punishing the rebel asserts and
vindicates the unity, the solidarity of mankind.   Of
course, the complete satirist never existed;   he
would, at any rate, be extra-human, and equally
of course, the human satirist, happily falling short
of his terrible ideal, is often not only a shrewd but
a kindly judge; but then the extent of his power is
proved in nothing better than in its abrupt cessation.
The perfect master of satire would not desire to
influence or in any way affect the strange vicissitudes
of things;   he would be content to record them,
and we should err in giving this title even to the
devil.

Yet so far as he succeeds in the achievement of
his plan, the satirist holds up a mirror in which the
world may see how odd a face it wears.   The orator
too holds up a mirror, but it is one in which men see
themselves not only as they are, but as they ought
to be, and smitten by the astounding contrast, turn
their abashed gaze inwards upon their own hearts
and there find, in a peaceful illumination, that
permanent self which they call an ideal, that ideal
which is the sum of things, reached not by addition
but by intelligence.   For oratory is action;   it is
a mode of living intense and yet comprehensive,
and the listeners are caught into the flow and
measure of a life which for the time at least is made
their own.   It has the effect of tragedy;   it purges

the mind. "Whatever," said St Augustine[1], "may
be the majesty of style, the life of the speaker will
count for more in securing the hearers' compliance."
But the life of the speaker is shared by the hearers.
St Augustine, well knowing the distance which
separates genuine from false sympathy, and aware
also, we need not doubt, of the enchantment which
a great speaker may exercise not only on his hearers
but upon himself, at times mistaking fluency or
impetuosity of speech for real inspiration, adds a
caution[2]—"The orator while he says what is just
and holy and good (and he ought never to say anything else) does all he can to be heard with intelligence, with pleasure, and with obedience." And
yet the whole meaning will not be at once or without
effort apprehended. The orator may be compared
to an athlete, well trained, and running a race; those
who try to accompany him over a part of his course
cannot expect to keep up with him even for a short
distance without great exertion; they will not attend
him to the long end, but they will not have wasted
their breath, if they become breathless, or their
exertion if they are very tired. "The very obscurity,"
St Augustine goes on, correcting his own advice, "of
these divine and wholesome words was a necessary
element in eloquence of a kind that was designed to
profit our understandings, not only by the discovery
of Truth, but by the exercise of their powers."
   Two more passages from the same writer will lead

---

[1] Augustine, *Christian Doctrine*, IV, xxvii.
[2] *Op. cit.* IV, xv.

us to a consideration with which this essay may be brought to an end.

"And yet the validity of logical sequences is not a thing devised by men, but is observed and noted by them that they may be able to learn and teach it; for it exists eternally in the reason of things, and has its origin with God[1]."

"For as there is a kind of eloquence that is more becoming in youth, and a kind that is more becoming in old age, and nothing can be called eloquence if it be not suitable to the person of the speaker, so there is a kind of eloquence that is becoming in men who justly claim the highest authority, and who are evidently inspired by God[2]."

If the orator, like some divine artificer, rejects nothing; if he is concerned to find order where there was incongruous disarray, if he is making the fragments of experience fit each other, and proves them parts of some coherent and systematised whole; if it is his singular task to render the parts intelligible to themselves, by giving them some understanding of the transcendent but simple unity of the total;— then it is less difficult to see why the name of his art, oratory, is another name for prayer. It is an art, "conveniens infirmitati nostrae." So St Hilary speaks of it: fit for our human imperfection; fit for it because fitting it to a completeness for which imperfection makes a claim that cannot be ignored,

---

[1] Augustine, *Christian Doctrine*, II, xxxii.
[2] *Op. cit.* IV, vi.

a completeness of which imperfection realised is the unfailing evidence.

Oratory, the moving language with which a great speaker seizes and sways his hearers, carries them upon the strong current of his own emotion, and persuades them that what he says is what they mean,—oratory by fashioning of common materials an ideal in which they discover themselves, and see themselves nobler creatures than they were before those compelling and transforming words touched their ears and caught their imagination, reconciles them to the world. It also reconciles the world to them. It is emotion, disciplined by laboured constraint, and rid by discipline of grossness; and guiding, in the light of experience enriched and irradiated by reflection, to action governed by cogent and temperate reason. At its utmost exaltation, though it is in the figure of ordered language that men have been willing to present it to themselves, it passes beyond the power of uttered words or argument; when the processes of reasoning are caught up and lost in a sublime conclusion, and speech, designed to make men intelligible to each other, to reconcile disputants, and still the noise of controversy, passes into an ineffable colloquy, the voiceless intercourse[1] of God and man.

[1] There too, logic, a tributary science, has its part. "'Come, let us reason together,' saith the Lord."

For EU product safety concerns, contact us at Calle de José Abascal, 56–1°,
28003 Madrid, Spain or eugpsr@cambridge.org.

www.ingramcontent.com/pod-product-compliance
Ingram Content Group UK Ltd.
Pitfield, Milton Keynes, MK11 3LW, UK
UKHW020313140625
459647UK00018B/1846